WILLIAM
Still Barking

Grace Dorey

Edited by Claire Makin

ryelands

To Nick, for giving me a bundle of fun.

*To Claire, Martin, Jo, Maggie and Charlie
for being the best family in the world.*

*To all those who believe that dog training is a walk in the
park and to those with experience who know it is not.*

Front cover: *Grace and William* (Photo courtesy of *North Devon Journal*)
Back cover: *William* (Photo by Allison O'Donoghue)

First published in Great Britain in 2009

British Library Cataloguing-in-Publication Data
A CIP record for this title is available from the British Library

ISBN 978 1 906551 17 9

RYELANDS
Halsgrove House,
Ryelands Industrial Estate,
Bagley Road, Wellington, Somerset TA21 9PZ
Tel: 01823 653777   Fax: 01823 216796
email: sales@halsgrove.com

Part of the Halsgrove group of companies
Information on all Halsgrove titles is available at: www.halsgrove.com

Printed and bound by The Short Run Press, Exeter

CONTENTS

ACKNOWLEDGEMENTS

My gratitude goes to Glennis Hewitson for breeding my beautiful pedigree Golden Retriever puppy and for kindly letting me have him despite serious reservations.

My thanks go to my daughter Claire, my son Martin, my daughter-in-law Jo, and my grand-daughters, Maggie and Charlie, for being so special.

I am indebted to my talented cousin, Claire Makin, for kindly agreeing to edit a second book.

Most importantly, I would like to thank Nick for chuckling each time I recounted William's triumphs and disasters, but most of all for encouraging me to write a sequel to *Barking Mad in Barnstaple*.

Grace Dorey

CHAPTER 1

IN THE FIRING LINE

FOR CHRISTMAS 2006, Nick kindly gave me the most adorable champagne-coloured bundle of fur. I named him William and I adored him from the day he was mine. How things have changed in only twelve months. My Golden Retriever is now the size of an adolescent elephant, and this year (among other wonderful presents) my nearest and dearest gave me a pet-friendly vacuum cleaner!

This generous present was in response to a chain of events that happened on Christmas Eve. My daughter, Claire, accidentally knocked a glass of red wine over my new, neutral-coloured wool carpet in the drawing room. Thoughtfully, she immediately soaked it with Nick's best white wine, and then for good measure sprinkled sea salt over the soggy patch, before assembling the vacuum cleaner in preparation for sucking salt from the offending area. But there seemed to be precious little suction, so she kindly decided to empty the plastic dust box and bang it clean outside.

Unknown to Claire, William sneaked off down the garden to chew the lid, which, when retrieved, resulted in a very dead vacuum cleaner with not a suck in sight. Nick immediately whisked me off to the shops, just before they closed for Christmas, to purchase a special 'pet' vacuum cleaner that was guaranteed to suck the most stubborn dog and cat fur from anything and everything. Among other things, it clearly also sucked up furry animals, as the instructions included the proviso: 'DO NOT USE ON YOUR PET'!

One day, the temptation to suck the muck from William became almost too overwhelming. Indeed, I could have defied the instructions there and then and sucked him right up inside my gleaming new red machine! I had left him outside in the garden with a chicken-filled bone while I ate my lunch in peace. But when I called him, shook the gravy bone box and whistled, there was no dog happily steaming up the garden towards me. I panicked. He had escaped! I popped on my Barbour to search the lane, just as my neighbour John, with a freshly-beating heart transplant, brought a very bedraggled dog to my five-barred gate. "Is this your dog?" he asked. "It looks too dark for yours." He returned one mucky, muddy muffin to an overly-grateful, grey granny and we proceeded to search for a possible William-sized hole in the fence. I barricaded a possible gap with a wire panel, returned to my cottage and promptly experienced the mother of all migraines.

When my eyesight returned, I started this diary as much-needed therapy and an alternative to emptying the wine cellar, or placing my pounding head in my gas-free Aga.

The next week, I met the local farmer. I was dining in The Chichester Arms at Bishops Tawton with Helen, the nurse who was staying in my converted barn. "Was it your dog who chased my chickens last week?" he asked. "My mother had to tie him up."

"Yes, I'm afraid it was," I confessed. "He escaped through a hole in the fence, but I've purchased twenty-five metres of wire stock fencing to prevent it happening again and am waiting for my gardener to fix it for me."

"Fine," he replied. "But next time he disturbs my chickens, I will shoot him".

I felt this was extraordinarily unfair, and particularly cruel as the chickens were not confined to his farm, but roamed all over the road and there was no farmyard gate to prevent dogs from entering the drive. He also threatened to shoot William if he chased the sheep in the neighbouring field.

Dear Diary, when will William behave? When? Nick generously gave William a large rubber-backed padded mat for Christmas. At first this was most acceptable to him as he stretched out on it each night with obvious gratitude and pleasure. It was a joy to vacuum. It lasted until the New Year when I arrived home one day to find my kitchen covered with white cotton wool padding, akin to a severe snow storm, that should still have been contained within the new green mat. William was most upset when I removed his bedding, and he tried feverishly to retrieve it before I could place it in the shed. Dogs are not meant to attack their beds. He had previously chewed the edging to his large green plastic bed, which I bought to match the Aga, so he had a pretty poor cot-care record.

A more impressive Christmas present from Nick was a fine stone sculpture of a dog, designed to sit proudly on the manhole-cover on my lawn. Even though it was delivered to the wrong manhole while I was out working, the reception it produced from William was spectacular. He initially looked scared stiff, then stood and barked loudly before cautiously creeping up to the sculpture. This timid display was followed by a series of woofs whilst bouncing backwards from each angle until he was brave enough to get close enough to sniff the sculpture's impressive genitals. Indeed he was dwarfed by this new arrival and obviously displeased to have some resident male competition. The barking continued each time he ventured into the garden for the next week. If only the sculpture could have barked back (or better still, have moved over to the correct manhole).

I now had problems. If I let him out in the garden, William would bark or, worse still, could escape. So I allowed him his freedom on The Green at Landkey. Unfortunately he became madly attracted to a furry rat-like creature being walked by a man wearing a navy-blue hood. I called "Come William" without success. I shouted "Come William" to my spirited pet, who was frankly annoying the yappy dog and his disgruntled owner. I bellowed "Come William" and whistled repeatedly, but they carried on ahead of me, intent on leaving the Green as soon as possible. I raced up as fast as I could, only to see them disappearing and heading for the road. Eventually, after risking heart failure, I caught up with William and put him on the lead, while the other dog owner shouted: "You should keep your dog on the lead, he almost got run over!". What possessed this man to leave the park and head for a busy road followed by an excitable dog, knowing that its owner was yelling its name! I found this behaviour extraordinary, but was too relieved to say how I really felt, which was: "You are a pillock, not a dog lover! Why didn't you wait for me to capture my dog?".

I mentioned this narrow escape to Glennis, my friend who

bred William, and she felt that the man was totally out of line. No dog lover would entice an unleashed dog onto a main road. This sorry episode resulted in me keeping William on the lead and not giving him his freedom in the park for fear of another similar event. Meanwhile, I was still paranoid that William would escape from my garden and get shot before Barry, my gardener, had constructed the fortress-style fence that I had designed. The last time I walked into the garden with Wills, he smelled the chickens and made a dash through the rather bare hedge. Fortunately I was close enough to save him from descending a 20-foot drop down to the road by tugging on his tail. I pulled him back in the manner of Pooh's friends, when they removed this loveable bear from his honey-pot. Indeed, I could have done with the help of both Eeyore and Owl! It was hard work lifting a large dog up a steep slope by his tail. Wills was extraordinarily phlegmatic about the situation and turned his head as if to say: "Thank you for saving my bacon. You really are a good sport.". If only he had learned his lesson there and then, I would have been able to sleep more comfortably at night.

It was not just chickens that excited William; it was any moving target. So when we were walking down the lane from my cottage, I instantly knew there was trouble ahead when I saw a young lady wheeling an infant in a pushchair down the hill towards us. To compound the problem, she was accompanied not only by a tiny back-combed dog but, horror of horrors, by her young son who was wobbling perilously on a fairy 'cycle. William bounced with glee and jumped up to pounce on one, or indeed all, of them. I asked him to sit. Nothing! I yelled at him "Sit". No reaction! He strained at his leash like a demented dog, while I had to use every fibre of my being plus everything I kept in reserve, to control him. Fortunately they carried on their walk unscathed, but only I knew what a close call it had been. I dreamed that night that I placed a lampshade around William's head to subdue my dog. When I woke in the morning, I mused that some of the best ideas in the world come in the dark hours from the distorted world of dreams.

On Valentine's Day 2008 I had owned William for one whole year (although he was my Christmas present, he became mine to take home on this special day). Judging by the scrapes he had dragged me into, this was a remarkably fine achievement. For the last three weeks, I had kept him restrained on the leash even in my own garden, for fear that he would escape and the farmer would carry out his cruel threat. At this stage, Barry, the gardener, was working feverishly twice a week to create a kind of canine Fort Knox using twenty fence posts and 100 metres of stock fencing. So for William's Valentine treat we met my friend, Hillary, at Fremington Quay for a walk along the Tarka Trail in the crisp February sunshine. Hillary brought along Sam, a beautiful freshly-brushed little Shih Tzu puppy, who was just seven months old. The previous night, I dreamed that William had eaten the puppy - fur, fluffy tail and all, and from that moment, I was unable to sleep as I agonized over whether I was sensible to let my rampant adolescent pup be within yards of little Sam.

I need not have worried. William sniffed Sam from stem to stern and then, satisfied, continued his bid for freedom by pulling heavily on the lead. As there was no-one in sight along the footpath, which stretched all the way to Barnstaple along a disused railway track, I slipped off his leash. For William all his Valentines had come at once. He ignored Sam and with one leap descended into the muddy ditch beside the trail and wallowed in it, before emerging as a happy dark brown dog with an expression designed to melt me. Sam was still pristine with his long white and grey fur swinging rhythmically with each dainty step. Apparently this breed does not moult fur all over the house, which is a definite bonus. In contrast, William's fur was caked in ditch-coloured mud giving him the look of an unkempt, unwashed, wild dingo.

As people walked towards him, I yelled to them in the manner of a fishwife with toothache: "Don't let him jump up, he's a puppy and he's filthy!". With the word 'puppy', dog lovers became intensely interested and gave him infinitely more attention than his lack of grooming deserved. He became a popular character, flashed his dark brown eyes at his audience and enjoyed all the unwarranted attention. He was in his element. He chased after each cyclist as they sped by, though they were fortunately able to outpace him and left him rushing and panting back to me. I need not have worried. The trail was safe and William was able to release all the pent up energy that had built up from his lack of freedom. Both dogs were placed in the back of their cars, parked carefully in the shade with the windows ajar, while Hillary and I were able to enjoy a delicious lunch in the restaurant. Both William and I slept happily that night and the mud brushed out well in the morning.

On February 20th 2008 my garden was deemed William-proof by Barry. William regained his freedom to roam around the half-acre. The posts and stock fencing and staples had cost £150 and Barry's time had added another £150 to the final bill of £300, which was worth every penny, if it prevented my dog from chasing the sheep and chickens and more importantly from being shot. That week the local paper carried a photograph on the front cover of a beautiful white cat from Barnstaple that had been shot in the head with an air rifle. This unfortunate cat suffered a miserable and agonizing time until he was eventually euthanised by the vet. The owners of the cat were bereft by the result of this savage act. I felt their agony and winced for William. My duty was to protect him and keep him safe and definitely off the front page of the local journal.

I was walking my infamous dog down the lane from my cottage, when William suddenly dived into the hedge raising a pheasant into the air. With one swoop, he leaped into the air like a jumbo-sized flying squirrel, missing the wily bird by inches, but with me in tow like an ungainly Mary Poppins hanging on to her black umbrella. He then continued the walk with his ears pricked up smelling every pheasant sized gap in the hedge expectantly, hoping to find a colony of similarly exciting prey.

Dogs seem to pounce on everything that moves. We are delighted when they catch a ball and even more thrilled when they bring it back to us. However I was far from delighted when William caught an adult grey wild rabbit, which was feeding innocently on my lawn totally unaware that danger was looming. With one accurate leap, William pounced upon his unsuspecting prey. When I walked slowly up to my errant dog, he held the rabbit in his mouth and swiftly ran away. He then carefully placed the unfortunate bunny back on the lawn and batted it about in an attempt to make it move. The rabbit squealed while my heart froze to have witnessed this abject and unnecessary cruelty. This merciless playing was repeated until the rabbit was lifeless, when I was at last able to drag my killer dog from his quarry. I know this is normal behaviour in the wild, but I would dearly love to have the ability to control my dog and tame this wild aggression.

This inborn desire to kill became all too evident during a visit to Dorset to see my brother, Alan, and his family. We arrived with William looking divine having been brushed and fluffed up for the occasion. This time, there was no hint of the travel incontinence or car sickness that he had experienced on his previous visit when he was a young puppy. We left for an immediate walk with my brother, sister-in-law, Rosemary, my niece, Anna, her husband, John, and my great niece, little Isabella, aged one-and-a-quarter accompanied by their Labrador, Tula, aged three years. Tula was amazingly obedient and put young William to shame. She came immediately when called and negotiated stiles adeptly, but more importantly walked beautifully to heel.

William on the other hand became madly excited and bouncy and within five minutes ventured into a freshly dug vegetable garden to hone his earth-turning skills. He bonded well with Tula when off the lead, but when he was on the lead he tugged my arm out of its socket in an effort to be top dog. Unsurprisingly, my family were suspicious as to whether he had ever attended any dog training. When we passed some peacock chicks, which were only a few days old and running across the path, I feared for their lives but somehow I managed to keep my attack hound sitting, albeit straining and slobbering a profuse amount of saliva.

When we arrived back at the house, Tula was still clean, needing only a little foot wipe. Wills on the other hand had leaped, sunk and rolled into every muddy puddle and was black from head to toe. Unsurprisingly he was not invited in, but was relegated to the boot of my car. How is it that one dog can cross muddy fields and stay pristine, while another one becomes caked in all the mud that Dorset can provide? Would he ever get over this stage or was he a compulsive puddle-fancier, destined to spend the rest of his life wallowing in the mud?

Meanwhile, across the Atlantic in Boston, my friend Liz's daughter, Kate found her missing Labrador, Henry, who had squeezed under the pool cover and sadly died under the ice. They had spent three weeks pinning up notices and enlisting all their friends to help find their much loved dog. He was the same age as Wills and my heart went out to Kate and the family, especially as in three days time Kate and John were getting married.

This appeared on the www.missinghenry.com website.

Henry
(August 2006 - March 2008)

Henry was found March 27, 2008 (he was missing for 17 days). He was found in the backyard pool which only had a small amount of frozen rain water in it. It was one of the first places everyone looked. Search teams gathered there several times in the past weeks and no one saw him because pool had been covered in ice and leaves. This is a sad and terrible lesson that we all had to learn the hard way. Please remember as we approach summer months, that pools (even just partially filled) are dangerous for kids and pets. We will miss Henry so much... but he is home now. Thank you all for your support.

John and Kate's wedding was then delayed for two weeks.

My friends Dorothy and Terry from Surrey lost their Retriever, Tara, when she chased a rabbit while they were walking across the Common. Days later, she was found in a railway tunnel having tragically been hit by a train. Tara's mother was my previous dog, Mischa, and the loss was enormous for all of us.

These unhappy events contributed to my fear that in a second, William could be harmed from any number of unfortunate and unpredictable events. It is a huge responsibility to own a dog and extraordinarily difficult to get the balance right between being over-protective and allowing exploratory freedom, rather in the same way that parents wrestle with either confining their children to set boundaries or allowing them to be free spirits to enjoy the countryside.

Since my garden was fenced, I have allowed William to have his freedom. Unfortunately this came at a price for the rabbit population. One windy gusty morning, he killed not one, but two adult bunnies using his tried and tested pouncing, playing and rolling routine. I have reassured myself that they were terminally ill with myxomatosis and needed culling, but I have a sneaking suspicion that they would have liked to spend their twilight years in my garden feeding from the lush verdant grass purporting to be my lawn.

It was on this wet soggy lawn that William was to have his photo shoot to grace the front cover for my book *Barking Mad in Barnstaple*. The publisher had agreed to print colour photographs on both covers and also inside the galley. My daughter was working tirelessly on puppy sketches to crown each chapter, based on a series of mobile 'phone snaps that I had taken throughout the first year of William's eventful life. My son, Martin, brought along his digital camera and chose the view of the hills as the perfect back drop. The photo shoot did not go to plan; William was not trained to sit in front of a camera with a cheesy smile and when he did get the hang of it, he posed with his tongue hanging out, which I understand is not how most supermodels behave. I then wanted him to appear 'Barking Mad', but there was little chance of this happening while he was bathed in the warmth of this rapturous attention. Then the battery on the camera died and with it any chance of getting the one perfect shot.

CHAPTER 2

KILLER INSTINCT

SPRING, WITH ITS attendant sap rising, bud bursting and leaf unfurling, spawns a multitude of crazy garden-improvement schemes. In my case, I had to keep my garden well and truly in tubs to prevent newly-planted flowers from being uprooted by my wilful hound, although I must say that this year, he had left the daffodils standing erect. In an enthusiastic moment, I visited the garden centre to replace the terracotta pot that was broken to pieces a few days before, when William danced, a tad too strenuously, with the window cleaner's little dog. I purchased two wooden tubs to take the two miniature evergreen trees that had stood impressively, until the accident, either side of the barn door. I paid £26.99 for each pot and came home to find a voucher in my purse allowing me (maddeningly) to have '£5 off' for pot purchases above £50. The next day I went back for two more tubs to be planted with lavender, but there was only one left. I went to the loveliest lady on the checkout and started to explain: "Before you say anything, yesterday I purchased two tubs for £53.98; here is the bill. I particularly came here because I have this voucher for £5; here it is. I wanted to buy another two tubs of this size but you only have one, so please can you kindly take £5 off this purchase?", I added breathlessly.

"Just a moment." said the kind lady. "I'm sure this is possible." She scrutinised the crumpled scrap of paper I offered. Then she said: "My dear, this voucher is for Homebase, you are in St John's Garden Centre!".

This year I have asked Barry to come along twice a week, as the garden seems to need more attention, mainly because I seem to spend so much of my time lecturing, which leaves little time for weeding. So when my next guest, Lyn, arrived the garden was looking delightful. Lyn brought her eight year old Boxer, Cassie, and I waited fearfully for two things to happen: firstly for William to sniff and mount his new lady friend, and secondly for him to attack. Neither happened! The dogs seemed fine together and after the normal investigative routine they seemed happy to play in the garden. In fact this year, Cassie stayed in the garden. Last year Lyn came to house-sit before my fence was dog proof, and Cassie escaped into the field leaving Lyn to climb over the fence and round up her over-excited dog. Fortunately there were no sheep in the field and no farmers brandishing firearms.

However, all was not so sweet in the house. Cassie scent-marked the kitchen floor, making a smell that reminded me of William's puppy days-days I preferred not to revisit. After I mopped up, it happened again and I cannot be sure that William did not add to the mess, though his urine was much stronger and there were no spray marks on the cupboards. Why do bitches do this? Was she marking her new territory or was she calling for male attention? There is no analogy in the human world. Female patients tell me that if they leak urine, it is off-putting to their partners except on the rare occasions when they lose control during sexual activity, when some men are turned on by this total abandonment and think it is a female ejaculation.

My new book titled *Love Your Gusset: Make friends with your pelvic floor* contains a cartoon of a woman spraying her partner during sexual intercourse; she is looking extremely flustered, while he is saying "Wow!". This little book became 'Book of the Week' in *The Mail on Sunday's 'You'* magazine, while I was on holiday with Nick in Ireland, which meant that I returned home to find orders for more than 400 books. For one whole week, I stuffed and stamped envelopes and rushed them down to the post office, until I hit on a plan to waylay the postman, when he was bringing me my mail, and to ask him to take the boxes of books down for me. This lovely lad, who wears shorts in all weathers, was only too happy to oblige.

In Ireland, Nick and I had stayed at Coopers Hill, a lovely Edwardian House in Rivertown, just South of Sligo. From there, we went house-hunting for the perfect house overlooking the sea. We visited most of the coastline from Easky to Bundora and were particularly impressed with the breathtaking views of the beautiful blue inlets, flanked by the stunning mountain scenery. We both fell in love with an Art Deco property at Strandridge, which was situated on the side of the mountain with glorious views of the bay and mountains beyond. Sadly it had already been sold, but that did not prevent me from dreaming of what might have been.

Simon, the owner of Coopers Hill was training a newly rescued Springer Spaniel puppy named Alice, who was seven months old and a perfect delight. It made me realise how much easier it was to handle a small dog, compared to controlling my large brute! Alice arrived in the elegant drawing room, when we were enjoying pre-dinner drinks, for her share of petting and cosseting, leaving an array of slippers, toys and bones in her wake. I would dearly have liked to kidnap this delightful puppy and bring her back home to Devon, though caution told me that William might enjoy his new playmate a little too much and we might be over-run with Span-trievers within nine weeks!

Before I left for Ireland, I presented my first *Advanced* Male Continence and Sexual Dysfunction Study Day in Cardiff for nurses and physiotherapists. One of the physiotherapy delegates was a delightful girl named Kirsty, who had been blind from birth. Indeed, she was married to a blind husband and fortunately had two normally-sighted children. She arrived with her blonde Labrador, Norman, who gently guided her to a seat in the front row. Norman sat on my toes while I was lecturing, a pleasure I had never experienced before! He was extremely obedient and so very different from my headstrong hound. Indeed, he could have taught Wills a few manners. However, I was delighted to report that even the perfectly-trained Norman had his moments. During the mid-morning break, he disappeared into the staff room and with one gulp deftly devoured all the Maltesers that had been thoughtfully laid out on the coffee table for the delegates! Dogs are not meant to eat chocolate, but when Kirsty was told about Norman's nibbling, she told us not to worry. This had happened before, she said, and he would be probably sick (hopefully not on my feet!). He retained the Maltesers for the whole course, and at each break scampered into the staff room in a fruitless quest for fresh supplies.

On arriving home, I immediately collected William from Springfield kennels. To my surprise and pride Linda reported that he had been awarded a gold star. I glowed in a similar way to how I had felt on Parents' Day, when my children had achieved distinguished work. Wills was growing up. All my hard work was paying off at last. Just as I was inwardly congratulating myself, John popped his head round the door and said: "Sorry, make that a silver star, he's bitten his orange plastic bed all round the edges!". Typical William, and the reason why his large, heavy-duty green plastic bed had to be removed at home.

But William was an angel compared with a Briard that arrived at Springfield Kennels. He spied John and Linda's ginger tom cat sitting proudly by their back door, and with one swift swoop, he lifted the far-from-fortunate feline into his mouth by the nape of her neck and sped round the field for three circuits before he lost interest and deposited the shocked pet onto the grass. Happily, the petrified puss was stunned but unharmed.

Back home, William rushed into the garden with the speed of a cheetah on heat and came back just as quickly to my kitchen door with a tiny, live, baby rabbit in his mouth. He would not drop it and ran away each time that I made a grab for his collar. This was too much for me. Linda from Springfield thought I ought to get an obnoxious-spray-collar to deter William, so I found one on the Internet for £165. It could be operated from a distance of 300 metres to spray a jet of citronella in the dog's face. It seemed that protecting my rabbits was a costly exercise, so I decided to think about it for a wee-while longer.

Nick thought that the problem could be solved more cheaply and effectively by using a water pistol. This should work, judging by the way William had kept a safe distance from the hosepipe, ever since I sprayed his nose and sent him leaping backwards indignantly, with the startled expression of an electrocuted hare. But where would I find a water pistol to contain the quantity of water that I required? Surely the toy shops were prevented by law from selling pistols that could contain enough water to drench parents. What I needed was a water-cannon like those used by the police, with enough volume to disperse a disreputable and disorderly mob - though I guess I would have to be careful in my enthusiasm not to drown the bunny that I was trying feverishly to save.

With thoughts of drowned rabbits, I took William to the vet

to see Harriet, who gave him puppy socialisation classes a year ago and introduced us to all the deadly parasites which abound in the wilds of North Devon. Harriet gave Wills a drop of kennel cough vaccine up the left nostril at a cost of £21 a drop! She also checked his chip, which was still firmly in place between his furry shoulders and warned me that if I was taking William abroad, I needed to check for the different pet travel requirements of each country. Possibly William would be travelling next to Ireland, a country with similar pet laws to our own, so he would be spared any further jabs. His anti-rabies vaccination lasted three years, and judging by how time flies, I was sure that this date would come round sooner than expected. At least he would not have to wait six months for the blood test results as he did last time.

Nick and I decided to sneak off to Brittany for a week; this time without William, as we expected to spend a good deal of the time shopping. Nick wanted to equip his kitchen in Ireland with some of the latest French kitchen appliances and gadgets that had so impressed us on our last visit to Morlaix. Wills was destined to spend his holiday at Springfield Kennels with John and Linda, who kindly let him play in their field with any suitable large male dog in residence and who would cope with the boundless energy of an over-ebullient adolescent.

Last year we took William to France for three weeks: in fact he *made* our holiday. He was a delight most of the time, but there were serious puppy moments when he became over-boisterous with the French, over-adventurous on the beaches and over-eager to dash off and disappear. At that time the holiday was 100% geared to the needs and training of a wilful puppy. It was fun and exasperating in equal measure, but etched in my mind for ever will be his raw excitement on reaching each deserted sandy beach in turn and undertaking a programme of feverish digging, as a prelude to performing a headstand in the freshly-dug hole, not so neatly followed by his spectacular self-choreographed somersault sequence. It was absolutely priceless!

I was concerned this year that I would pine for my best friend when we left him behind, particularly if we walked on any of the beaches that we visited last year. I knew I would miss him to bits. However it was impossible to take him this time. Nick was sailing over from Ireland and I was flying from

Exeter to Rennes, where Nick was kindly meeting me. We were not staying at a dog friendly gîte this time, but at the impressive Manoir du Sphinx at Perros-Guirec overlooking the islands and boulders of the pink granite coast. I guessed that however dog friendly the French purported to be, this 'bonhomie' did not extend to English dogs the size of a bull elephant, likely to rampage through their chic hotels! So William was booked into a classy kennel with the promise of "Maybe next time, sport".

William will be one-and-a-half years old next month. He is a wonderful companion who gets me out of bed with a series of guttural whines building up to a loud 'Woof' and greets me by nuzzling close to my legs with his tail wagging, like a windmill whizzing around in windy weather. I pop on my dressing gown and take him out on a heavy duty lead to his favourite nettle bed; the one that smells right for him to pee. This programme takes a few minutes and is usually followed by William rushing back to the kitchen and me leaping back to bed! On wet days, when all smells disappear, he takes for ever, sniffing every wild weed in an effort to find the correct smelling plants to water, or indeed a plant with any scent at all. Hence I have some thriving nettles and towering tares all watered willingly by Wills. It surprises me how he gets among the nettles and cocks his leg without stinging his precious penis.

I can remember when I was a little girl in a skimpy sundress and my father was showing me how to fly a box kite. I held on to the string and moved backwards, until I vanished completely from view in a stinging nettle ditch! I can still remember how the discomfort felt like a million, trillion wasp stings. When I went to Brownies later that day, my mother had to tell Brown Owl that I did not have chicken pox! When there are no nettles, William will squat like a girl in the long grass, for longer than usual, letting the weeds tickle his manhood, while he looks at me with an expression of pure joy, as if this is one of the principal pleasures of life. I think he would stay there for ever if he had a good book!

I love the expression he makes when he smells chicken, sees eggs or spots a bottle of milk. If I make a cup of tea for a visitor, he will bark for his share of the milk. His floppy ears rise at the base giving his face a wider, manly, more maddeningly-attractive look. I also particularly love the look that he gives me when he is holding a large meat bone. His jowls overhang the bone making his face widen appealingly, while his eyes look as if he is in canine heaven. Another of his special expressions he saves for when I command him to "Sit" before food, and then "Wait" when he expectantly shows me the white crescent below his deep brown eyes, until I say "OK". This routine has become a habit for both of us. He needs my approval before he can commence eating and is willing to submit to me, mainly because I am the provider of food and have alpha or top dog status in this closely-knit pack of two.

My alpha standing allows me to decide where or when we walk. If I pop William on the leash, he knows we will be walking down the lane and turns right on leaving the kitchen. He waits patiently while I look in the post-box on the gate for any letters, even though the post-man may have handed them to me personally earlier! He knows to keep to the left going down the hill, cross the road when I say "Over", and then come back up the hill still hugging the left hedge. This perfect sequence can be changed at a moment's notice by a number of unexpected disruptions such as the scent of a mouse, the fluttering of a bird in the hedgerow or, worse still, the sight of a new born lamb through the gate to the field, when I have to hang on to his lead as if I am holding a ferocious attack-bull. If a car speeds past I first ask him nicely to sit, then I yell " Sit!" until I get the desired reaction - and then have to hold him firmly to prevent him chasing the car that has passed.

According to Wikipedia, 'the on-line fount of all knowledge', Golden Retrievers are renowned for their intelligence, and can learn up to 240 commands, words and phrases. I counted how many words William could understand. He reacted correctly to the commands of: "Come William", "Sit", "Wait", "Down", "Stay", "Do you want to go for a walk?", "Over", "Home", and "In" most of the time, but he still had his maddening, melting moments of sheer puppy-mindedness. And he had yet to learn a mere 231 commands! What on earth were these important words, phrases or even songs? No doubt Goldie owners across Britain were having newspapers, cups of tea and even gin and tonics brought to them by their faithful friends. I was obviously missing out on being pampered, by an under-performing pet. William had much to learn.

On one of his training expeditions down the lane, Wills almost tugged the extra-strong lead out of my hand and dived into a waxy plant. He came out with a mouse, half of which he devoured instantly, while the freshly-bitten tail end dropped out of his mouth onto the ground. When I pulled him away, he dashed back with the strength of a well-toned tug-of-war team and gobbled up the rest in one greedy gulp.

William's doggy memory meant that our walks took longer each day. He always nosed into the part of the hedge that served as the pheasant's launch pad, then he was eager to reach the gate in case there was another baby lamb waiting for a fatal frolic, before he reached the waxy plant, hoping for another modest mouse meal.

If I let him out into the garden without a lead he turns left and cursorily watches for my consent before dashing down the garden to chase any bird, rabbit or leaf that has the impudence to move. He becomes as wild as a bouncing, pouncing tiger if any lamb strays near the border to the field, and jumps up repeatedly in an attempt to clear the fence and fly cleanly over like a champion racehorse with wings. I always watch him when he is in the garden for fear of him leaping over or tunnelling under the new fence. I am still extremely nervous that if he happens to escape, the farmer will shoot him even though the sheep belong to his tenant.

Dogs have an inbuilt desire to spread their wings and fly away. I read in 'The Daily Telegraph' that Harvey, a three-year-old Staffordshire bull terrier, had mastered the art of jumping on a trampoline with a four-year-old girl named Chloe. One day, the terrier used this newly-acquired skill to bounce his way clean over the neighbour's fence to freedom and was eventually found, three days later, a mile away.

CHAPTER 3

A FURRY TALE

I TOOK WILLS down to the Green at Landkey and met Toby for the first time. Toby was a gorgeous seven month old male Golden Retriever, who sported the most fabulous silky puppy fur, which swung softly with every bouncing step and, even more alluringly, was a joy to stroke. William's fur has become thicker and coarser since he has lost his puppy fluff. Toby was about half the size of my monster, a fact which left his owner fearful that in a few short months he would grow to these gigantic proportions. Toby was altogether a more controlled and less physical chap, who not only stayed close to his mistress, but was one of those miracle dogs who stay clean. Wills on the other hand took the opportunity to dive into his favourite muddy ditch and emerged dark brown from the tips of his paws to his long painted eyelashes, with spattered specks of something very unsavoury over his ears. I persuaded William to dive into the river to rinse himself clean, but unhappily this cleansing programme was followed by another leap into the quagmire! Just at the time I thought Toby should be safely tucked up in bed, we met him again. He was still swinging his unsullied hips, while William's nether regions were black, wet and matted from a thousand efflu-ents. As Wills flashed a wicked look at Toby, I shrugged with resignation knowing that Toby would not be allowed out to play with my mischief-maker. No-one loves a dirty dog - not even his owner!

When I collected William from his holiday kennels after our French trip, John gave me an excellent report on his conduct and progress. He thought that my overgrown puppy was turning into a fine and controllable dog (even though they still called him 'Just William'!), who came when he was called and who played happily with the other dogs. By way of a test, we let William out of the field into the unfenced front garden without a lead, in preparation for jumping into the car. He circled the car sniffing everything within reach, before springing nimbly in. What a star, and another example of how he could behave in front of an expectant, even adoring, audience. On arriving home, William re-acquainted himself with the garden by sniffing every leaf, twig and blade of grass, before scent-marking the perimeter with urine in an effort to make it smell more homely. Where does all this urine come from? Does this mean that he always has a full bladder? In humans it is considered harmful to retain urine; why is it not harmful for dogs, especially as the urine of male dogs is so strong?

As the garden looked powder dry, I unwound the hosepipe in preparation for soaking the tubs of fuchsias and lavender and the bed of pink hydrangeas which, this year, were accompanied by an amazing array of wild pale pink foxgloves. Any floral interloper is made welcome as long as it is pink! Last year, the hydrangea bed was filled with a mass of wild, double, pink poppies, but this year they must have been harvested by a succession of totally unsporting hungry bunnies. These ravenous rabbits had devoured every single one. This reminded me of the time when I visited Claire, my daughter, who was then living in Amsterdam, where she kept a house-rabbit. On her birthday, her boyfriend generously gave her a dozen red roses. When we returned from dinner that night, every leaf had been stripped clean by the rabbit, who must have mounted the sofa and leapt about three feet onto the occasional table to reach the vase of flowers. Only the rose buds and stalks defiantly remained.

William ran around the garden keeping well clear of the hose, obviously remembering the time when he was a young pup and I spurted a warning jet of water onto his nose. He indignantly leapt into the air as if attempting to jump over the moon in reverse. There was no doubt, after William's week in the kennels, that he needed much more reassurance in the form of stroking, cuddling and cosseting. This renewed bonding is always a two way process, which defines how much we both desire to be needed and loved.

I have just read the courageous book *A Three Dog Life* by

Abigail Thomas, who was comforted by her three dogs after her husband tragically sustained a head injury when the leash snapped while he was walking one of their dogs, and he tried to save it from running under a car. When she was on her own, Abigail found that the company of her dogs gave her great solace, particularly when they slept with her at night. At the front of her book, she cites a wonderful Wikipedia quotation: "Australian Aboriginies slept with their dogs for warmth on cold nights, the coldest being a 'three dog night'!". I guess if it was likely to be chilly, you threw another dog on the bed! Perhaps this is the origin of our duvet tog-rating system. Personally, and with no offence to William, I prefer a dog-less duvet. Imagine what would happen if Nick found Wills occupying his side of the bed!

In fact, I kept William in the kitchen, as it was easy to vacuum up the dog hair that seemed to drift, swirl and spread everywhere at an alarming rate every time he twitched, even though he was combed every day. Judging by the amount of fur collected on the comb, I was surprised he was not as bald as a frog. I can understand people who prefer short-haired dogs, which do not moult, but I loved the look and feel of his long hair, which was truly silky and sensuous. I have heard that some women knit dog-fur into jumpers; if I knew where they lived, I could happily supply the odd ton. Wills will stand to be combed from the top of his head to the tip of his tail, if I am lucky, but he far prefers to lie on his back proudly showing his manhood so that I can comb his legs and tummy-fur while he purrs in pure exalted, exquisitely enraptured ecstasy.

At last I had a use for William's fur - not the fur he was wearing, to which he was rather attached, but the hair that was left matted on the comb. I was having a section of the cob on my 16th Century cottage re-rendered after a metre-square patch of lime plaster was blown off in February's severe storm. Clearly, this was an insurance issue and, two loss adjustors later, a satisfactory conclusion was reached after the last guy adjusted himself and scaled the roof of my cottage in his immaculate dark pin-striped suit and pink tie, putting the dress code of my army of builders to shame! This kind man, Rob, took an instant liking to William, and cosseted him until his smart city suit was covered in enough cream dog-fur to excite his Golden Retriever bitch when he arrived home! Maybe in his own inimitable way, William helped to settle this claim favourably.

The lime render was always mixed with horse hair to make it bind to the cob, which was made from lime and cow dung a staggering 500 years ago. The builder asked for William's hair to help strengthen the lime. Indeed, William should be able to supplement his pocket money now every time he is groomed, and although his coat is not as coarse as a horse's, it is comforting to know that he has helped to strengthen the wall to my cottage for the next half Millennium. Not many dogs leave that unique legacy.

CHAPTER 4

LIFE AND DEATH

CANCER IS THE most common cause of mortality in Golden Retrievers, according to The Golden Retriever Club of America's National Health Survey: 1998-1999. My last pet, Mischa, had to be euthanised as she was suffering from cancer of the spleen, which, the vet informed me, could have burst at any time. She was five years old when I took her on, so I had seven wonderful years with her before the finality of her death dealt such a sad and heart-achingly cruel blow. I can understand why some people are put off from ever owning another dog, being unable to go through this abject anguish again.

I felt that if I brought up a puppy I would have the privilege of being with my dog, hopefully, for twelve years.

Some dogs have a sense of impending and inevitable doom. One treasured dog, who had slowly limped up stairs with great difficulty for years, one night suddenly rushed up stairs and licked each member of the household as they slept, before rushing downstairs to die.

Another was not so prescient. This was an unfortunate Jack Russell who was fed wild mushrooms at a dinner party. When the poor dog keeled over and died in front of the esteemed guests, the hapless hostess telephoned 999 and they were all advised to attend the local hospital to have their stomachs pumped.

I read in *The Daily Telegraph* that the world's oldest dog is 36 years old! If William attained that exalted age, I would be knocking on 102 years of age before he joins Mischa in canine paradise. Not a pleasing thought! I don't think there is much to commend getting older. One has to develop a sense of humour to be able to cope with all that smacks life in the face, like the untimely loss of memory, the tiredness and the lack of enthusi-

asm for anyone or anything that fails to enhance life's sweet tap-
estry. Television programmes are carefully selected for their
sense of humour; nothing tacky or rude, but those with a clever
sense of the outrageously absurd that are actually funny, even
though they may contain the odd anti-Christian expletive.

Life changes with the passing of years. I have enjoyed each
stage of the journey and would not wish to retrace my tracks.
On a bad day, I find it amusing when my joints grumble to such
an extent that I get out of a chair like a geriatric giraffe on a skid
pan. On a good day, I rush round the tennis court with an elderly
group of over 50s who, in their prime, were all champions and
who now make up for their lack of speed with a medley of cunningly executed shots. I value Nick's love and loyalty and I feel
contented and comfortable knowing how much he cares. My
friends have become increasingly important; all chosen for the
helping of humour that they happily provide.

My future lies with my children and grandchildren, in whose
company I am happy to spend more and more time. I never
realised the huge bond that exists between a grandmother and
her grand-daughters, before they arrived. In my eyes they are
perfect and are the only folk in the world who can get away with
saying: "Gran Gran, why is your hair white at the front and black
at the back, when it used to be yellow like mine?", and: "Gran
Gran, you look funny without your glasses", and even: "The skin
on the back of your hands is baggy; it goes smooth when you
bend your fingers. You must always keep both hands in a fist"!

And then there is William, my best friend and, I hope, pro-
tector, who is a fount of unlimited hilarity, which I cannot keep
to myself, but must recount to any mad dog-lovers who will
listen. His entertainment value is priceless.

I am fearful that William may escape, become disorientated
and get run over. Ever since I saw him disappearing out of sight
following a Frenchman jogging with his two Goldies in Brittany,
I have been concerned that he could be stolen. I then came across
a Pet Locator on the internet, which is lightweight, waterproof
and durable and traces your pet precisely using satellite signals
- all for £74.99. This device would have helped locate my friend's
Golden Retriever, Tara – the dog who chased a rabbit into a
railway tunnel and was tragically hit by a train,and was not discovered for a week; also my friend's Labrador, Henry – the dog
who was missing for 17 days before they unhappily found him

under the ice in their swimming pool. I decided to think about it and discuss it with Nick. If William became lost, I would forever wish that I had bought this device. I was curious to know the size and weight of the tracking equipment I would be expected to carry about and the effective operating distance. Further exploration on the internet revealed that the device, which attaches to a dog's collar, is about the size of a mobile 'phone, that the GPS system needs a zone pre-set, and that the owner is alerted by a text message or email. The downside is that you need to pay a $9.99 monthly service charge, though there are a plethora of practical possibilities. You could use the device to track your pet, your Porsche or even your partner!

The next guests in the Barn, Kelvin and Helen, had recently lost their treasured Golden Retriever bitch, Saffron, and in contrast to some holiday-makers, who do not understand or want to understand the intricacies of dog behaviour, were delighted to meet another Goldie. Kelvin in particular lay down in the drive with William, ruffling his fur, while both of them purred in mutual ecstasy. It was a pleasure to watch. He then asked if he could take William for a walk. In the evening, Nick telephoned from Norway where he was salmon fishing, and playfully suggested that my holidaymakers might want to take William home with them. I remembered how I had wanted to take Alice, the rescued Springer puppy, home with me.

That night I had the darkest nightmare. My precious dog had been kidnapped and I was in the middle of a rough housing estate yelling "William" and vainly listening for his bark while scanning all the windows for a glimpse of his cream fur. I dialled 999 on my mobile 'phone and alerted the police to the dastardly crime, which they considered to be a very low priority, sending me cleanly off the anxiety scale until I woke up drenched in sweat, trembling, feeling bereft and distraught.

It is incredible how dreams can bring your fears to the surface and disturb your contented and carefree existence. The next day Kelvin asked if he could take William for a walk. I reluctantly agreed, but could not help myself from issuing enough instructions to fill a canine manual: "Please keep him on the lead", "He walks on the left", "Mind the lorries", "He'll pull when he sees the farmyard dog", I recited like a hopeless, lovelorn lunatic. It was like handing over a beloved child to the responsibility of a teacher on his first day at school. While they were away, I worried unreasonably about William's safety, remembering all too vividly the time when I was on holiday in Brittany walking Ann and John's dog, Alphonse, when he was hit by a car. Fortunately he recovered, but the shock of this accident will always be deeply imprinted in my memory. My stress level soared skywards until I saw Wills coming up the hill towards my cottage walking happily to heel, having enjoyed a romp by the river with his new friend. I need not have worried. William was turning into a fine dog.

Kelvin later told me that during their holiday their love for William, coupled with his playfulness, had been instrumental in their decision to have another dog. However, they decided against having a male dog, as they disliked his habit of marking his territory every five minutes. They returned home to seek out a Golden Retriever bitch: just the kind of mate that William would like to take on! Quick as a cunning cobra, he immediately invited them to come to stay in the Barn next year.

I told my friend, Jeanine, that William was now settling down. After the havoc that he caused last year in her garden, in just under two hours, when he nearly floored a man with a broken ankle and then disappeared into a trough of water, 16 feet deep, I could tell that Jeanine did not even slightly believe me. She told me that she was now taking her dog, Clyde, to visit her ninety-one year old aunt in a residential home and was delighted to be asked if her pet could join the 'Pat-a-Dog' scheme and bring joy to the homebound residents.

I mentioned that William would enjoy all this attention, but Jeanine swiftly assured me that he would not be ready until he was 12 years old! So Clyde is now enjoying regular charity work and is proudly paid in pats. This reminded me of the time when I was in Australia and had a much treasured photograph taken while I was cuddling a koala. These friendly marsupials are solid and quite heavy to hold, but they cling to you as if you are the only one they love. Indeed, these cuties are either jolly good actors or they crave human attention. I thought then what a great life they were having, being available for cuddles for two hours a day - a kind of dream ticket. Then I read in the paper that the Wildlife Park was going to stop this delightful custom, because it was unkind to the koalas! I bet they took umbrage and sulked. I would have turned my back on humanity and stayed up my eucalyptus tree for days.

CHAPTER 5

ILL-GOTTEN GAINS

THE NEXT GUESTS in the barn arrived with two pale Golden Retriever bitches, who fortunately were not in season. Bonnie was a playful two-year-old whilst Ellie had slowed down considerably in advance of her nine years of age. William was in his element and immediately bonded with Bonnie, and they romped through my garden as if they were Siamese twins, rolling on my not-so-hardy annuals and generally running amok. While the dogs were blissfully tiring themselves out, their owners, Mr and Mrs Whitehart, told me about the Beagle they used to own. This little guy used to jump out of an upstairs window and roam for miles. If they took him for a walk, he would be attached to a clothes line. If he escaped, they would see the white tip of his tail wagging happily miles away, before he arrived home and let himself in straight through the glass panel on their front door! On occasions he would arrive home in a Black Maria.

"I bet the Police loved him," I said. "Well no," Mr Whitehart replied. "When he was chained up, he scratched all their patrol cars!"

The Whiteharts were adamant that they would never, ever, have another Beagle, but believed that Goldies were the perfect pets. They said that by staggering the ages of the dogs, the older one would train the younger one. Clearly, I realized where I had gone wrong: William should have had a father figure to knock him into shape!

One dog took a lead from a trio of cats, to his detriment. In *The Daily Telegraph* there was a sorry photograph of an adolescent Dogue de Bordeaux, named Moses, who had followed three cats out through the cat-flap in their front door. This escapade culminated in him getting his head firmly and immoveably stuck.

When his owner returned from shopping, she saw the funny side of this calamity and rang the fire brigade who released her monster 13.5 stone hound dog. I bet he rushed back into his Moses basket and hid in shame.

While Moses was becoming unstuck, I had to attend a Urology Meeting in Arlington, Virginia, so I left William at Springfield Kennels, his alternative and (I think) preferred accommodation. I drove up to Heathrow firmly believing that all would be well, now that he was growing up to be such a fine chap. This was a whistle stop visit to America, where I was spending just two days lecturing, but all the more enjoyable because I could cross the pond on a Virgin Atlantic bed on the same flight as my nephew, Chris, who was travelling back home to Arlington. It was a delight to visit him one evening and relax with his beautiful wife, Heidi, and their lovely children, Rowan and Pippa, and catch up on all their news. On the way home I broke my journey in Bristol to supervise my PhD student, Christine, who was at the crucial writing-up stage of her thesis.

I arrived at Springfield to collect Wills. "Did William behave himself?" I asked out of politeness, not expecting for a minute to receive a negative reply. I was invited inside the house by John, who shut the door tightly before giving me my pet's poor progress report. Apparently Murphy, a large brown Labrador, had been busy humping all the other big dogs in the field and when he was taken back to his kennel early, due to his un-gentlemanly tendencies, William mimicked his mating behaviour with gusto. For the rest of the stay William performed 'a Murphy' on all the other male dogs, until he had to be separated and relegated to sad solitary exercise sessions.

As John was relating this story, accompanied by a series of very visual thrusting motions whilst traversing the room, I tried desperately to keep my face from cracking and maintain the composure expected of an elderly, and I hoped, sophisticated lady - until I could not cope a moment longer and we both laughed hopelessly, helplessly and wholeheartedly. The mighty Murphy had turned my muffin into an over-generous, gay sex maniac!

As I left with my rampant dog, John gave me some advice. "There's no need to have him castrated as this behaviour may settle down, but do be careful when there are children about," he warned. Ashamedly, I paid the fee for William's pleasurable stay and took my sex-kitten home.

On the trip to America, I had read a book that my daughter, Claire, had kindly given me, as she knows that I am a sucker for doggy books and thought that my canine library was incomplete. It was called *A Dog Year* by Jon Katz, and was the book that had inspired John Grogan to write his best seller *Marley and Me*. Jon relates the colourful story of a Border Collie puppy, called Devon, who had been sadly ill-treated for the first six months of life and was sent to him by a female friend to be 'straightened out', as she knew he already owned two extremely placid and well-trained Labradors.

Young Devon arrived at the airport in a crate, where Jon was introduced to a black and white bit of fluff, resembling a Catherine wheel, who circled his cage at high speed, spinning like a harassed hamster in a hurry. As his new owner opened the crate to fix his lead, the wild demon sprung out like a bullet, necessitating five airport officials to track him down and eventually catch him! On arriving home, Jon sensibly decided to take the Labradors out first, as they walked to heel without a leash, leaving young Devon secure in the yard. While Jon was walking down front path with the Labs, Devon made a dash for freedom and escaped before totally disappearing from view, until suddenly there was a flash of black and white sitting on the top of a mini-van travelling slowly down the street! Even Wills had not topped this troublesome behaviour.

William, however, had his own plans. Claire arrived from London for the weekend, wearing some snazzy new yellow shoes with 'high-as-you-please' heels bought the previous day from Selfridges. No sooner had she taken them off than William seized the opportunity to hurtle into the garden with a delicious mouthful of lemon leather. I rushed out with the box of his favourite liver-filled biscuits, which failed to tempt his palate or indeed gain his attention at all. Claire turned the air navy blue with her screaming, which only seemed to make him more excitable and infinitely more determined to hang onto his ill-gotten gain. Eventually after a series of circuits of the lawn, my electrically-charged monster released the shoe in an attempt to hoover up some or all of the biscuits, leaving Claire with a soggy, tooth-marked shoe, which resembled something that the dog had chewed. The moral of this story had to be: 'Leave your designer shoes in London when you visit a dog with a fiendish leather fetish'.

'DO NOT LEAVE ANYTHING WITHIN REACH OF THIS ATTACK DOG' might have been more appropriate. We humans will never learn – at least, I don't. The very next day after the shoe incident, I was delighted to hear that the Conservation Planning Permission had been granted for moving my office into the Barn loft and for creating an 'en suite' bathroom. Excitedly I looked up the builder's details and telephoned him to see how early he could start this project. After the call, I returned to the kitchen to find that William the Impossible had ripped my address book to pieces and it was lying on the floor, looking more like a soggy papier-mâché apology than a book in a readable form. It took an evening's work armed with a roll of sticky tape to patch it up. As I was trying to piece all the addresses and telephone numbers together, I thought of the man whose wife had shredded all his love letters and used them to stuff a cushion. After her death, he spent 15 years piecing them together, so that he could write a book about their love story. I, on the other hand, was not feeling boundless love for either my hound nor, for that matter, for myself for leaving my address book within his reach.

I decided to have my cottage lime-washed after it had been re-plastered following severe storm damage to the gable end. William was intrigued by all the builders who arrived, but even more by the selection of rubber gloves, paint brushes and items of clothing left lying about. This was heaven-sent for Wills, who helped himself to a number of trophies and managed to disrupt and delay each day's proceedings. I went out one day with the required number of cups of tea (those with sugar and those without) and, horror of horrors, I saw a bucket of white-wash tipped over on its side, pouring out all over my patio. Wills was suspect number one. I will never know if he had been too curious or if the tub of paint had just turned over in the breeze. I used two dog towels to clear up the mess (poetic justice) and a strong jet of water from the hosepipe. William, as always, skulked and hid when the hose was being used, but coupled with his water-jet fear, I am sure I detected a tiny tweak of guilt.

My son Martin telephoned me to ask what Nick and I thought about his family owning a Springer Spaniel, as they had just been to visit a friend with a new litter and the children had been excitedly enthralled. I remembered Alice, the perfect puppy, and said that it was a lovely idea for the children to have a pet. Nick reminded Martin that Springers need a lot of exercising, but Martin said he knew this, and it was part of the reason why he wanted a puppy. I was very pleased that they did not choose a Jack Russell like Paddy the Fearless, biter of ankles and champion ratter, their previous dog who was now earning his keep on a farm. Recently, Paddy had fallen into the silage pit at the farm and had to be saved from a ghastly death by Freddie, the quick-thinking farmer. The next day this spirited canine survivor was trampled on by some cows that had bolted, and sustained a very squashed foot, but that evening, true to form, despite his injuries, he caught another delicacy to add to his collection of rat-tailed trophies.

Later, I cottoned on to the fact that the new and as yet unnamed puppy would be left with me when the family were away, and I wondered whether William would be unsettled by this intrusion. Would he see it as prey and annihilate the new arrival? Would he become frisky and hump the wee thing (possible)? Would he become the dominant male and teach him how to behave (unlikely)? Or would he extend the hand of friendship and enjoy romping with a new playmate (preferred)? I gave Martin the dog cage from Nick's Range Rover, and he gratefully took this home to assemble in preparation for the new arrival. He then fashioned a set of shelves for the girls' room so that their belongings could be put out of harm's way. I told him the story of my shredded address book as a cautionary tale, but their minds were well and truly made up. The puppy was on its way.

The next week Martin telephoned me to say that the puppy was ready for collection; even though it was still tiny and decidedly delicate, as the largest in the litter, it was surely going to survive. The puppy cost £250, but surprisingly had not received any of the statutory inoculations. Martin was going to name him Bob or Frank - to be frank he was undecided. This wee puppy was destined to be walked off his tiny feet once he had received a few pricks and was allowed loose in the Devon countryside and beyond.

CHAPTER 6

A FAN FROM OZ

W HEN I WAS in Rome for the publication of my six self-help books translated into Italian, and lecturing to nurses in 37 degrees Centigrade, I met a talented nurse from Adelaide, who became an actress before turning to journalism. She was bravely undertaking a European tour on her own, with thoughts of writing a book about her many diverse adventures. One evening in a wonderful moaning session that would have done 'Grumpy Old Women' proud, we commiserated about the lack of air-conditioning and total absence of catering facilities in our crummy hotel. When she hit Portugal, she emailed me to say that her purse, containing her credit cards and 50 Euros, had been stolen from her room. I immediately emailed back to say: "Come down to 'pick-pocket-free' Devon for the weekend and I will show you around".

I collected Allison from Tiverton Parkway station, where she alighted from the train dragging a red suitcase that was so large that it looked as if she would be with me forever. The first night over a bottle of wine (each), she described, with journalistic accuracy, the difficulties (many) and joys (few) of travelling alone. The next day was gloriously sunny, so I took Allison and William to the beautiful and unspoiled resort of Saunton Sands, with its three miles of golden sands, where it was a staggering £6 to park the car. I was paranoid that William might display the wicked side to his nature on a beach scattered with family members of all shapes and sizes. I had visions of him jumping on the under-clad infants, of humping all the other dogs with little consideration for their feelings or gender, and of disappearing. In fact, amazingly, none of this happened.

True, he pulled so strongly to reach the beach that I had to release his lead. He was congratulated for thoughtfully depositing a large pile of poo close to the dog waste bin, making it considerably more convenient to clear up. He then visited each of the holiday-makers who were strolling along the sands, in an effort to receive a pat or nuzzle or just simply to chat. He looked amazingly handsome and elicited a number of fabulously favourable responses like: "I've left my dog at home with my Mother, but he is just lovely", "Isn't he soft?", and "What a beautiful dog!". William was standing erect and proud, while I, just as proudly, bathed in the reflected glory. He is after all an exceptionally good-looking dog. He bounded up to other free-running dogs and played happily with them, without a hint of any sexual pleasure. He was a joy to be with. Every time I called "William, come", he came back to me. It was extraordinary and so unlike my former wayward hound.

When we left the beach, we headed to The Thatch Inn garden at Croyde for lunch, where William sat happily tied to a wooden table, noisily emptying his water bowl. In the afternoon we visited Croyde Beach and throughout the walk, which traversed a camp-site, a river and enough sand to satisfy his digging genes, I called his name just to be sure that this new behaviour had not worn off. Every time I called, he bounded back to me. He had become a different dog; one who was a pleasure to be with; one who would have been warmly welcomed by the 'Pat-a-dog' scheme. In fact he was the kind of dog I wanted. We returned to the pub for a thirst-quenching drink and found the only table in the shade happened to be next to the children's play area. William, even in his sodden, sandy and rather sorry state, was surrounded by a host of 'little people', some who were considerably smaller in stature than himself, all eagerly waiting to stroke this fine dog. The climbing frame and slides were abandoned; William became the focus of toddler attention and sat happily receiving his petting with a misty-eyed expression designed to melt his many mini-masseurs.

I had parked the car in the car park opposite the pub. When we neared the road, I asked William to sit so that I could attach his lead. All went well until Allison crossed the road ahead of William, where the path disappears into the road on a narrow bend. It was a black spot; Allison beckoned me to cross, but I was fearful as I could not see either way and, like children, dogs pick up on their owner's fear, so William almost tugged my arm off in an effort to join her. I was distraught. A kind four-wheel-driver stopped on a sixpence for us to cross, before she wound down her window and called out: "I have one like that at home!" Now, crossing the road safely has to be the next important lesson that William has to master, if he intends to reach adulthood.

We then paid the acceptable road toll of £1.50p to visit Crow Point, a beautiful sandy spot bordering the river Taw, where a number of assorted dogs partied near the water's edge. William gate-crashed this event and joined in the games until I called. Again there was instant recognition and an obedient dog bounded back to me. I was impressed and staggered in equal measure. That evening, we celebrated Wills's new found obedience with a bottle of wine (one between two).

Early the next day I took Allison to visit Clovelly, a unique village that dates back to the 11th Century and that is owned by one man. Here, an assortment of beautiful cottages occupies a splendid deep valley terminating at the water's edge with a picturesque quay and harbour wall. We left William at home, as dogs have to be kept on leads in the village, but mainly because I did not fancy being tugged down all those smooth-rounded and often slippery cobble steps, even though it would have been good to have had a pull back up the steep hill. There was red, white and blue bunting displayed on every period house announcing that it was Lifeboat Day and a number of eclectic and vibrant stalls on the quaint quayside. All the villagers including the owner of the village and the Harbour Master were there supporting the event.

We popped into the Red Lion Hotel for a Cornish pasty (essential fare for overseas visitors) before feebly paying £2 each for a welcome lift up the hill by the jeep, which had fortunately replaced the donkey service. There were two elderly ladies in the Land Rover with us, before we were joined by a young couple. When Allison remarked that they were young enough to walk up the hill, the girl announced: "I am using pregnancy as my excuse", so the rest of us agreed that it was our excuse as well!

In order to complete the visit, Allison suggested that we should go to Hoops Inn for a cream tea, a delight that is well recommended to those visiting Devon. Once inside this exquisite, thatched pub, we were told that we would have to wait until 3.30pm. It was 3pm. How long does it take to knock up a pot of tea and a few scones? Indignantly, we proceeded to Tesco's and bought the necessary ingredients: leaf tea, fresh sultana scones, Cornish clotted cream and the finest strawberry jam. With no thought of the calories that would cling to our hips, possibly forever, we laid the table with a clean cloth and used the best china to enjoy this indulgent Devon ritual, while William, always one to benefit from any new situation, licked the clotted cream carton clean.

On Monday morning I took Allison and her jumbo, jam-packed, and similarly coloured trunk to Tiverton station to begin her long journey back to Australia. I hoped that I had been able to show her a sprinkling of Devon seventh-heaven and that she would want to return. I apologised for not providing five-a-day fruit and vegetables and explained that the local diet was slightly more varied than pasties and scones. She took some stunning photographs of this glorious part of Devon, which she intended to use both in her book (which I would love to read) and in her journalistic work. We had a great time, but on the trip to Tiverton, she started missing William, my pride and joy, who had cleverly recruited the first overseas member to his fan club. In fact, Allison left saying that she could not wait to read *Barking Mad in Barnstaple* when it was published in September and hear about his life as a delinquent and dozy puppy. William had scored!

CHAPTER 7

OF GNOMES AND OTHER PETS

I WENT OVER TO Martin and Jo's house to collect Maggie, now five years old and Charlie, now a grown-up four, for a visit to the Gnome Reserve close to Bradworthy. At the front door, I was met by Bob, the new arrival, a beautiful black 'Springer Spaniel' with a fluffy white chest. "We call that a white bib," said Maggie accurately. On closer examination this delightful puppy was not pure Springer; his ears looked more Labrador than Spaniel and his marking was definitely not that of a well-bred Springer. They had been sold a pup! But one who was the cutest, warmest, most adorable pet in the world. He loved all the fondling from the children as they lifted him into a variety of un-puppy-like poses. To be honest, I would have been happy to forgo the gnomes and play puppy for the rest of the day. However, the children were eager to visit the Gnome Reserve and Fairy Meadow so, after washing our hands, we set off.

It was a delight, as always, to spend time with my grand-children and to share their enthusiasm and excitement. They loved seeing the gnomes that they had remembered from our previous visit, and were delighted to discover some new little fellows that had mysteriously crept in. They ran round the Reserve three times, stopping at intervals to point out old and new wizened little men in a variety of scenes such as the orchestra, the chess board, the fishermen, the bathers, and the motor-cycle circuit. I asked the children to place their hands over their eyes and to tell me how many gnomes they remembered. After reciting the names of most of the models that we had seen, Charlie asked plaintively: "Please Gran Gran, can I take my hands away from my eyes now!".

Next, the children raced off towards the swings and demanded to be pushed higher and higher, which worried me with good reason. I explained to the girls that when their Daddy was their age, I pushed him right out of his swing! Undaunted they said they would hold on tight (just as he had promised me all those years before). I curbed my enthusiasm and they stayed seated! After lunch, we drifted around the Fairy Meadow, stopping to play in the house for little people, before finding seven out of the nine fairies complete with fairy wings (two must have flown away).

I drove back to their house, but found an outsized oil tanker blocking my route. "Don't worry," said Maggie. "I will direct you to my home." And she did! At five years of age, she was better than Sat Nav! When I delivered the children safely back home, Bob was asleep in his cage. I felt cheated. How could he sleep through the noise of both children talking at once, recounting their adventure to their mother? I promised to see Bob soon, hugged the family farewell and went home to William.

Later I read in *The Daily Telegraph* that a reckless law graduate named Simon had stolen an 8lb garden gnome and taken it on a world tour. Murphy, the leprechaun, was eventually returned to the owners after seven months with an album containing photographs of the gnome, showing him resplendent in South Africa, Swaziland, New Zealand, Australia, Singapore, Thailand, Cambodia, Vietnam, China, Hong Kong and Laos. Simon explained to the cheered owners that the gnome had left because he had itchy feet!

The next day (08/08/08) I had an appointment with Anne Tattersall, a freelance journalist working for *The North Devon Journal*. She had wanted to compile a feature on my sculptures to link with the article that she had recently written about Ron Machin, who was the model for one of my bronzes. I popped William in the car with the windows wide open so he would not jump on her, only to find that she loved dogs and had recently rescued two kicked and tormented Collie puppies. I learned from Anne that people who treat animals cruelly often go on to abuse their family members. This delightful lady not only gave her pets a charmed existence, but also gave her free time to the North Devon Hospice raising funds to help to make 'letting go' as comfortable an experience as possible for dying patients and their relatives. A truly remarkable woman.

While I was showing Anne my works in bronze, she noticed my self-help books, for men and women with incontinence and sexual dysfunction, lying on the table ready for distribution. Suddenly all interest in my sculptures evaporated, even Tarka the Otter, that she had stroked and found so sensuous was sidelined, and she asked if she could let her readers know about my books. "These should be available on the NHS for every man who undergoes prostate surgery and every woman who has a baby; this preventive approach could save them a fortune in providing incontinence pads and even surgery in later life," she announced with great insight. Excitedly, I told her that my latest book was about the trials and tribulations of training my delinquent dog and his immature bladder! Later that day she emailed a manuscript for me to check for accuracy. She had written 1,000 words on the way in which my books could provide information on pelvic floor exercises to spare men and women the embarrassment of urinary leakage and sexual dysfunction, but rounded off her article announcing the imminent publication of *Barking Mad in Barnstaple*! William was on his way to stardom.

A delightful photographer called Tom duly arrived from the *North Devon Journal* to take a photograph of William (with me) to accompany Anne's article in Tatt's Life. Previously Anne wanted a shot of me with my bronze sculpture of Ron Machin, but now the goalpost had changed. In a twinkling of an eyelid, my furry friend in his quintessential quest for glory had cunningly ousted Ron! Tom was enlisted because he loved dogs. I brushed my hound and turned to the photographer.

"I thought you should never work with children or animals," I said. "It's the humans who are the most difficult!", he replied. So I tried to be easy, but the resulting photograph made me look like William's twin sister, further supporting the theory that people look like their dogs!

William's new-found fame did not prevent him from bounding up to my next Barn visitors, Andy and Emma, who were accompanied by their Golden Retriever, Merlin. William had met this fine dog last year when he (Wills) was an uncontrolled and boisterous puppy. Merlin had been booted out from Guide Dogs for the Blind, due to hip dysplasia and was now more than happily re-homed. This fully trained and decidedly docile dog arrived wearing a large cumbersome lampshade and, if that was not enough, his left hind leg was tightly bandaged. He had undergone surgery to remove a cancerous lump at the top of his left foreleg, so had to wear a shade and bandage to prevent him from scratching the stitched wound. He was only six years old.

William rushed off down the garden with Merlin in full battle gear sweeping away everything in his path. I wondered if William remembered being forced to wear similar plastic apparel when his paw had been bitten by an overzealous Airdale. Wills must have felt a good deal of sympathy, but unfortunately this was laced with a tad of rumbustious superiority.

On a day of relentless rain, I met Glennis with her granddaughter, Jordan, for afternoon tea at St John's Garden Centre. Glennis told me that one of her friends had taken her Goldie to the dunes at Saunton Sands the previous day, when it was bitten by an adder. Fortunately the dog had been able to walk back to the car and reach the vet in time for an injection of antidote. Oh, to be in Ireland where there are no snakes!

When I was bragging, yes bragging, to Glennis about William's new found obedience on Saunton Sands and beyond, Jordan piped up: "Frankie is so naughty now. He jumps up on all the other dogs." So this Champion dog, William's brother, was going through a similar pattern of male adolescence. This was like nectar to my ears, as it was the first time that Frankie had offended (apart from the chewing through the outlet pipe to Glennis's washing machine which flooded her kitchen with soapy water). I now found that, instead of zooming in on the all-too-frequent felonies Wills had committed, I was venting his vainglorious virtues. I was becoming a proud puppy possessor!

I was praising my dog's improved behaviour to Sally. I had called to give her a lift to Jennie's new house in Bude for dinner, for what happened to be a hilarious evening, as always, with my two sex therapy friends. When I arrived at Sally's house I was met by Tiki, a seven month old Labradoodle (Labrador/Poodle cross), a 'pedigree' which is not yet recognised by the Kennel Club of Great Britain. This beautiful curly black puppy was just gorgeous, but still not completely accepted by their sleek two year old black Labrador, Zed. Their Lab was beautifully trained and among her many talents she knew to stay out of the kitchen when the family were eating.

If a cross between a male lion and a tigress is a 'liger' and the cross between a male tiger and a lioness is a 'tigon', surely a Labradoodle must have a Labrador father and a Poodle mother. But what is the cross between a Poodle father and Labrador mother? Is it a Poodlab?

On the way home I started moaning about the decorators who were painting the outside of my cottage, as the owner of the company had been verbally abusive and threatening. I also mentioned that William had developed a new habit of barking for milk every time that I put the kettle on to make the painters a cup of tea, and that he now preferred his dry food with a little milk. Sally mentioned that cow's milk is particularly bad for dogs and that she would email her family member who was a vet. He kindly sent this email:

Adult animals are not good at digesting milk and it can cause problems (allergies, enteritis, etc.). They are best with water and can easily be weaned off milk by simply providing water rather than milk (dogs don't understand the cold turkey concept, so are not phased by this approach). If she really wants to, she can dilute the milk a bit more every day until it becomes just water but this is treating the owner and not the dog so it's your area of expertise not mine.

So William would have to learn that he was not allowed to have a drop every time I take milk out of the refrigerator. I wondered if the barking would stop or if, every time he spies milk, he will be 'still barking'!

CHAPTER 8

BARKING MAD
IN THE SHOPS

ON 12TH AUGUST 2008 *Barking Mad in Barnstaple* was published. When publisher Steven Pugsley telephoned me, my knees started to wobble. I sat down as my joints turned to junket. Why does excitement make your knees weaken? I had published 10 medical books without so much of a leg-jerking tremble. What was different this time? Pure emotion. I had candidly detailed a year of my life as I wrestled in an attempt to make my beloved puppy behave. It was a book about William, my new soul-mate, whom I adore despite (and because of) his enigmatic eccentricities.

The book was published much sooner than expected, as I had been given the estimated time of publication as late September. I immediately sent a blind email to the 400 people on my mailing list, causing my server to faint from exhaustion. The wooziness turned into a crash; sorry Virgin Mail. I could still send emails but, maddeningly, I was unable to receive the (favourable, I hoped) comments from my friends and colleagues. I also quickly found out which of the email addresses were redundant and who was happily away on holiday, as I received multiple recorded messages to this effect. Undaunted, I posted a book to Nick in Ireland and all the members of my extended family, whether they were dog lovers or not.

I took Martin and Jo's copy over when I baby-sat for Maggie and Charlie (and Bob, the puppy, who was now looking more Lab than Spaniel). The girls were now past babyhood, so were fun and easy to care for. Bob, however, was a different problem. He pee-ed on the carpet while I was trying to unlock the garden door, then repeated the exercise again before depositing something more solid on the lounge carpet. When I popped him in the cage, he whined; when he was allowed out, he jumped over the sofa then dragged a large red beanbag along the floor, like an ant hell-bent on dragging a prized sack of sugar back home. This little guy was like Tarzan. He was chosen because he was the strongest, liveliest lad in the litter but he was going to be a determinedly headstrong character. I was very pleased that I did not have to train him! He would have been shipped off to Boarding School until he was an adult!

I sold a book (my first) to my Barn guests, Andy and Emma, mainly, I think, because I told them that their dog Merlin's visit last year was featured in one of the chapters. Two minutes later, Emma popped her head round the door: "Please could I purchase another book, because we are arguing about who is going to read it first"!

Andy had invited his brother and sister-in-law down to the Barn for his brother's 50th birthday. To celebrate this auspicious occasion, he decked the outside of the barn with an array of brightly-coloured balloons. William was intrigued and frightened in equal measure. He approached the inflated display cautiously, before barking vehemently as if to alert the whole of Barnstaple to impending danger. How much was fear and how much was protection, I shall never know, but I have a sneaking suspicion that it was 1% alerting me to doom and 99% pure scaredy-pants.

The next day Merlin limped back to the Barn with a fresh bandage on his left hind leg. Apparently he had scratched off his old bandage revealing a very infected paw. After a £50 visit to the vet, he had been diagnosed with embedded grass seeds which, horror of horrors, had started to germinate. So Merlin was collar-bound for a good deal longer, back on stronger medication and, even worse, banned from frequenting the long grass. William visited his sick, subdued, no longer playful friend and offered him sincere, heartfelt sympathy, before running off triumphantly with Merlin's squeaky new bone.

My daughter Claire arrived with her boyfriend, Neil, for her birthday weekend. William immediately forgot about missing Merlin and swiftly switched his affections to Claire, who had always been his favourite. I gave her a copy of *Barking Mad in Barnstaple* which she wanted me to sign. She was delighted to see her illustrations in print and to read the acknowledgements. Neil asked if he could have a copy too, so I presented him with his own edition, duly signed. After dinner, Nick telephoned so I took the call upstairs for privacy, leaving the others in the kitchen (hopefully, to do the washing up). I came downstairs to find the most unholy mess, not just in the sink, but on the floor, where the dog's blanket was covered with chewed white paper balls. It was Neil's precious book! William had given us his own impression of my writing; in fact he was the first canine critic - it was fun, tasty, and eminently chewable!

I love being in my cottage in the summer. In this lovely setting, I feel close to nature. The gardener, who comes twice a week, has kept my garden trimmed, weeded and looking beautiful: I am indebted to him. In order not to upset his nearest and dearest, I had to stop myself from writing in his Christmas card that I could not live without him! I am woken each morning to scratching in the roof over my bed by a family of sparrows, one of which was sadly carried off by a sparrow-hawk flapping determinedly in the hedge opposite my kitchen door. I have a family of swallows nesting in the eaves, making a ghastly mess on my white, newly-painted, cob wall. They were forgiven for all the unsightly detritus when I saw four little fluffy heads poking out from their cleverly built mud nest. When I walked past, all four babies flew off at once and perched on my electricity cable in preparation for dobbing my blue car with white blobs. When William goes into the garden, the mother swallow flies low letting him chase her around the garden, like a turbo-charged Ferrari on a race track, always keeping slightly ahead before she flies up, up and away having attracted him away from the nest. She then returns to the overhead cables and neatly provides evidence of being shit-scared by blobbing my car!

This debacle was nothing compared with the excrement produced by a frightened baby swallow that flew into my house and christened the expensive John Lewis sofa in the Conservatory, not to mention the walls, the floor and the window sills. He kept flapping, crapping and snapping his head against the windows in his quest to fly out. I opened the door and a large window, but unfortunately failed to see my intruder leave, so despite searching every swallow-sized corner of the room, I had the sneaking suspicion, that he was still there, somewhere, out of sight in a very concussed and unhappy state.

The next car destined to be swallow-targeted brought my friend, Claire, and her delightful family: her son Angus, aged

12, and identical twin daughters, Poppy and Sophie (my god-daughter), aged 10. The children continuously used a superlative that was new to me; anything that had been 'wonderful', 'fabulous', 'super' or 'cool' in my day was now deemed 'funky', and William was thus named. We took my funky friend with us on the private road to Crow Point, where the children enjoyed being bounced about in the back of my car by the numerous road humps, while I was fearful for the health and well-being of my exhaust pipe. It was one of those days when mad dogs and Englishmen take cagoules and just 'go'. William was in his element, running with the children and chasing other dogs, topped only by sliding competitions down the large sand dune cliff which bordered the beach. I, of course, was silently on adder patrol and prevented any of the party from venturing deep into the dunes. We walked into the drizzle-soaked wind with sand abrasively lashing our faces, providing a free skin-peeling service, until we turned the corner towards the three-mile stretch of sand which, on a sunny day, forms the spectacular Saunton Sands.

We were buffeted all the way back to the car by biting wind and horizontal rain on our backs, pushing us home and making our return trip almost pleasurable! All would have been well if William had not taken a shine to a black dog of unknown parentage, who was happily walking into the gale in the opposite direction and attracting my pedigree pooch like a mega-magnet. "Come William," I hollered. "William," I yelled, while they rolled together in the quicksand, but unfortunately this majestic bellow fizzled to an inaudible whisper in the wind. William almost disappeared from view. Resignedly, I backtracked, getting increasingly wet and growing grumpier by the minute. Eventually, he turned and sped back to us, the colour of molten pitch, expecting a warm and wonderful welcome. Instead, on arriving home, he was rewarded with a good dowsing down.

The following day William was soft, silky and sweet smelling and in fine fettle after his compulsory bath. The children wanted to try go-karting in the morning (for some reason, William was not invited), and in the afternoon we took everyone to Instow, just as the holiday weather was worsening from pure unkind to downright ridiculous. As we set off across the sand in the driving mist, William produced an unpleasant offering, which I niftily scooped up in a plastic bag, asking Claire to watch

William while I walked back to the dog bin. William had other ideas. He followed me, then leapt over the wall onto the pavement. I was terrified that he would run into the road, so I called out to some holiday-makers who were walking along the pavement: "Please could you catch my puppy?" One of the ladies took hold of his neck, while I thanked her, and gratefully secured his lead. "How old is he?" her husband asked incredulously. I replied that he was 18 months, but not fully trained - which was, after all, alarmingly obvious.

Having captured my pet, I was able to release him back on the sand. He started to seek out the sandcastles that tiny holiday-makers had laboriously designed earlier in the day, before rolling over them in an attempt to 'kill' them. Where the children had dug holes, he continued the process until he was almost out of sight. He ran alongside Angus, Poppy and Sophie, then left them standing by rushing towards the sea to chase seagulls without a prayer of catching them. We were all completely oblivious to the electrically-charged elements. The beach darkened under a thick black cloud, the rain started to soak our faces and, worse still, penetrated our trousers, until we were completely sodden, so we shrieked and ran like frantic over-sized lemmings for shelter in the car.

The following week, my friends David and Gina came for lunch on their way back from a week spent with their family in Cornwall. David used to head up the Training Centre for Guide Dogs for the Blind in Leamington Spa, so it was no surprise, when he used his considerable knowledge and experience to state: "William is a handsome dog, who resembles a failed Guide Dog!" Not one of the best compliments that Wills has enjoyed, but one that was resoundingly accurate. I told them about the local obedience classes coupled with the expensive boarding school in Wales; in fact, about all my determined efforts to train the perfect puppy. They smiled a knowing smile before rushing home to read chapter and verse in his book.

I had a kind card from Merlin's owners, Andy and Emma, saying how much they had enjoyed reading *Barking Mad in Barnstaple* and asking me to send them the press clipping from 'Tatt's Life' in *The North Devon Journal*, when it was published. Merlin had had his stitches out and fortunately the prognosis was good. Andy and Emma then asked to place an order for William's next book!

Above: William with Jordan. (Photograph by Glennis Hewitson)

Below: Grace with wounded finger and young William, Eve, Emily and baby Amber. (Photograph by Rosemary Blundell)

Above: The sculpture of a large dog in the garden. William in the car in preparation for a walk. (Photo by Allison O'Donoghue)

Below: Grace and William. (Photo courtesy of North Devon Journal)

Above left: William at Towsers. (Photo by Sue Blackmore)

Above right: William – a critic of Barking Mad in Barnstaple.

Below: William paddling at Croyde Bay. (Photo by Allison O'Donoghue)

Above: Bob. (Photo by Martin Dorey)

Below: William digging under the garden fence in a bid for freedom. (Photo by Allison O'Donoghue)

CHAPTER 9

LIFE IN DEVON

O N 26/8/08 I had lived in Devon for 10 years. From the day that I arrived, I had felt as if I was on holiday. No more exhausting full-time work. No more waking to the alarm clock at 6.30am. No more fighting the traffic on the M25 on my way to work. No more staying late until the work was done. I moved to Devon to complete my Masters degree researching the treatment of male incontinence, but enjoyed studying so much that I embarked on my PhD researching 'Pelvic floor exercises for erectile dysfunction' at the University of the West of England, Bristol. This research proved to be so significant that I have been invited to all corners of the globe to present lectures and study days.

To mark this special day I bought a trashy Sunday paper, a packet of chocolate biscuits, and took William to Landkey for a walk. There he met Sasha, a three-year-old tiny Springer Spaniel with unlimited energy and the speed of a recently released Whippet. William chased her in ever increasing circles until part of the circle splashed in and out of the river; never catching her, but never giving up either. Their excitement intensified exponentially with each circuit, until they looked more like a drowned cat and mouse than playful domestic dogs. In the car travelling home, my soaked soulmate was happy, but smelt like a farmyard, sounded like a terminal heart-lung machine with emphysema, and looked like a goldfish with a limited supply of oxygen. In the kitchen, he lapped his water bowl dry (twice), then collapsed on his belly with all four legs outstretched to each of the points of the compass giving an impersonation of a fuzzy starfish, before giving me a look of exhausted contentment. A perfect celebration of the last decade!

Glennis popped in to purchase four signed books for the friends with whom she would be staying in Australia. She had been invited to judge the Golden Retriever section in the International Dog Show held in Perth; a huge honour. I gave her a few of my increasing collection of doggie books to read on the plane, particularly recommending *Amazing Gracie* by Dan Dye and Mark Beckloff as a totally absorbing read and one that would lose thousands of flying hours. This book tells the story of a pathetic white Great Dane puppy, the runt of the litter, who was destined to be destroyed because she was completely deaf. Gracie, who was taken in by Dan and Mark, was loved by everyone except their two resident, severely territorial Labradors. She eventually changed the lives of her owners, when they tempted her to eat by trying and failing with most dog-designed delicacies, until the vet suggested making home-made dog biscuits. This hobby quickly became a thriving organic, additive-free business, successfully enhanced by the allure and magnetism of the graceful shop assistant, Gracie. I wished Glennis a wonderful trip, told her not to worry that her daughter was having puppies while she was away and thanked her for being such a good friend these past ten years.

I had known Glennis for a decade. The day after I moved in, I walked down the lane from my cottage with my daughter, Claire, and noticed a large sign proclaiming "CATTERY" on my next door neighbour's cottage. As I had just lost Rosie, my gorgeous Persian tortoiseshell cat, we decided to knock on the door to see if, by chance, they had any kittens to keep me company. What happened next was truly unexpected. We were met by six extremely excited Golden Retrievers, who were exceptionally eager to meet their new neighbour. Their owner, Glennis, explained that they were no longer running the cattery, but that she bred Golden Retrievers. All my life I had been devoted to cats and had, to date, enjoyed the company of Picky, Smoky, Whisky, Ruffles, Oscar and Rosie. In a magical flash, I changed my allegiance from cats to dogs, as I had always promised myself a dog when I retired. Amazingly, I left my kind neighbour's house with Mischa, a five year old bitch who was 'ready for re-homing' mainly because she barked when anyone arrived and set off the rest of the pack.

For seven years, I cared for Mischa and she cared for me, mainly by barking to alert me to the arrival of any friend, foe or delivery. When I went away, Glennis and her husband, Derek, looked after her for me. The first time I left Mischa with them, she escaped from their cottage, causing much consternation and panic. They searched their property, the fields and the lanes, and eventually found her sitting on the doorstep of her new home, showing everyone in her own inimitable dog language exactly how very well she had settled in. And it happened the next time too, though that time they knew where to look! Mischa would walk down the lane without a lead; if I heard a vehicle, I called her and she would immediately come back to me. If I put her on the lead, she pulled, unless she was walking uphill, when the lead would go disappointingly limp!

She was great company. While I was studying for my PhD I would bash the keyboard of my computer mercilessly for two hours, then take her for a walk around the lanes, while I was alleviating all the stiffness in my back, neck and fingers and, more importantly, processing my thoughts into chapters for my thesis. This regime continued throughout my studies and enabled us both to get some much needed exercise and precious time together; Mischa was walked off her dainty feet. She never needed to have her claws clipped; she filed them down on the roads.

For three years, I paid no council tax as my cottage became a 'student house'. I saw few friends, treated research patients in my clinics, and read only urology books, journals and papers; looking back, I was completely driven to attaining my goal, knowing that it was possible only if I completed the necessary amount of work. I am forever grateful to my supervisors, Dr Margaret Miers, Mr Mark Speakman, Professor Roger Feneley, Professor Chris Dunn and Dr Annette Swinkels for their wisdom, experience and guidance in helping me to achieve a dream that I never thought was possible, until the day I stood in Bristol Cathedral in a red gown and black soft hat, complete with tassel, in front of Nick and my family, to proudly receive my doctorate.

Mischa and I were a team right up until the fateful day when she was diagnosed with cancer of the spleen, and I was told very, very gently by the kindest of vets, that the prognosis was bleak. After an agonising decision, supported by my nearest and dearest, dear Mischa was laid to rest. One half of our team departed leaving me totally bereft. It was one of the saddest and most emotional days of my life. The emptiness and the loneliness continued for weeks, stretching into months, in fact right up until the day when William arrived, filling my life with sunshine, occasional drizzle, flashes of brilliance and lightening storms. Mischa would have loved him.

William fluffed himself up in readiness to meet Bob, Martin and Jo's new puppy, whom they now believed had a terrier father (Bob had grown a beard!) and a Springer Spaniel mother, and which entitled them to receive a rebate of £100. I went with Jo, my grand-daughters Maggie and Charlie, and two dogs of disproportionate size to Peppercombe beach. We went over the cliffs in order to avoid a field of cows and found the most slippery mud in North Devon, possibly in the world; mud that was coloured red and looked and felt just like my smooth modelling clay. It was a miracle that the four of us on two legs stayed upright, though we had a few near misses; the two chaps on four legs had no problem and skimmed past us as they raced to the sea.

We arrived at the beach just in time for the tide to come in and flood over the top of the children's little red-riding-hood boots, leaving them to squelch their way back up the hill. Despite the size discrepancy, William and Bob were fine together; every so often they became aware of each other, when William jumped over Bob or pawed him gently into submission. Bob lay down belly-up in a classic submissive pose, which was surprising given the huge size of Wills towering above him. William was King, but for how long?

On the way back up the hill, where the path cut through some brambles, Charlie disappeared. I turned round to speak to her and she was gone. I called loudly and repeatedly and received no reply. Nothing. I guessed that she could be hiding and keeping quiet about her whereabouts. Why do we play hide-and-seek with children? I panicked the way one does when a child goes missing. Had someone carried her off? Maggie and I went along a bramble track to find her, but it was William who spotted her retracing her steps down the hill towards the sea. The relief was instant. I thanked William for being so clever, then gently explained to Charlie that I thought she was lost for ever and that she should not play tricks like that again. She held my hand so tightly after that, while William pulled us both up the hill.

The path traversed a field of cows. Well, there were two black cows sitting down watching us pass. But they were each the size of a recumbent elephant! I held William tightly on the lead hoping that he would not spook and disturb them from their digestive processing. All was well as we bravely walked on the path a few feet away from them; William was curious, but maybe too tired to get excited. It had been a long and tiring walk for all of us (we were even too late for lunch in the local pub), so we were glad to arrive back to Jo's house to replace our fluid loss and enjoy a light lunch.

The next morning my four-legged alarm clock was too shattered to bark, which meant that I woke up late at 8am and had to rush in the manner of a Mad March Hare to North Devon District Hospital to commence my morning Continence Clinic. At the hospital shop, I purchased a copy of *The North Devon Journal* to find a photograph of me and my twin, William, on page 48 together with Anne's write up under the heading: 'Snigger all you like, but Grace knows pelvic floors are no laughing matter'. The article listed all the self-help books that I had published along with my new book about William. Under the photograph by Tom Teegan, the caption read: 'A professor's best friend: Grace and a now well-behaved William', which was not strictly accurate, but sounded fantastic! If only! Even more impressive was that Gerri, the receptionist from the Ladywell Unit at the hospital, had seen our book *Barking Mad in Barnstaple* displayed for sale in St John's Garden Centre. We had made it onto the shelves!

CHAPTER 10

TICK ATTACK

I REGULARLY PLAY tennis at two tennis clubs, one indoor and one outdoor, though I far prefer to play indoors, where I am uninterrupted by the elements, be they rain, wind or even dazzling sunshine. The day that the local paper was published, I played outside at Barnstaple Bowling, Croquet and Tennis Club (no less) to find that most of my retired friends had already reached page 48. William was swiftly becoming a celebrity; he had gained notoriety by misbehaving. Was that the way to achieve such status? To judge by the standards of the tabloid press, detailing the antics of modern day 'celebrities', he had sinned well enough and often enough to become infamous. And more importantly he was photogenic.

Trelawney Garden Centre invited both William and me to a book signing on October 4th for three hours. Immediately, I anticipated the raw mayhem that wily, wild William could whip up in a winkling within the Pet Section. I despaired and telephoned Glennis to share my problem; she readily agreed to accompany me, possibly because she did not wish to miss the free entertainment that was sure to ensue!

While William was waiting for his grand debut, he honed his hunting skills by rushing into the garden like a recently released whippet, catching a baby rabbit and bringing a very dead specimen back to my kitchen steps for my approval. I was not pleased, but possibly not as displeased as the rabbit or its friends and relations. The family who dance on my lawn giving me so much pleasure and entertainment will be in mourning for days. Hopefully they will learn the much-needed lesson to play elsewhere, in order to stay away from my attack son-of-a-wolf, with his eagle eyes, beagle nose and cheetah-like speed.

Meanwhile, for a change, something was busily attacking William. It was pay back time! A thirsty tick had settled on his nose and was greedily helping himself to his life's blood. Last time he had a tick on his head, I twisted the interloper violently to remove it, leaving a disfiguring lump which was obvious for many weeks. At that time, Glennis gave me a piece of advice: "Put nail varnish remover on it; it will drop off immediately", so this time I dowsed the little devil with a nail varnish remover pad. William was indignant; he objected to the smell so close to his nasal passages. I chased him round the kitchen and after a few ineffectual circuits, with one awkward manoeuvre, I managed to free him from his leech-like parasite.

Rather too late, I treated Wills to a much-needed dose of anti-tick and anti-flea lotion, which stated clearly on the packet: "Treat every 4 weeks for ticks". So it was my fault that William had been attacked. I read about these blood-suckers on the web and was informed about the danger of Lyme Disease from a tick bite; it emphasized that if he developed an infection, he should have early treatment with antibiotics. I found a picture of a sheep tick, Ixodes ricinus, which was identical to William's invader. I apologised to my pal and promised to be more diligent in the future. I even wrote: "For tick treatment" in my diary in a month's time. Even better, the first day of the month became 'Tick day'.

The next morning I noticed a pool of blood on the floor. On further examination, I discovered that I had trodden on an engorged tick, which must have dropped from William's body following his treatment. I searched for further evidence and found another fat fiend on the floor. What surprised me was that I had not felt these beasts when I had cosseted and combed William; they had remained craftily concealed. I always combed him each day with a wire rake. Recently there was much more fur on the comb and multiple tufts on the floor. I should have noticed that he was scratching more; I thought he was just going through a seasonal moult and worried in case he would be bald for his book signing! These little devils had burrowed under Wills's curly, long fur and remained craftily hidden, while they surreptitiously sucked their supper.

I learned that Lyme disease occurs not only in dogs, but

can also be transmitted to humans by the bite of an infected tick. The disease was named in 1975, after a number of cases occurred in Old Lyme, Connecticut. The offending bacterium 'borrelia burgdorferi sensu lato' can cause fever, headache, fatigue and a skin rash called 'erythema migrans' diagnosed by red circles surrounding the bite. If left untreated, it can affect the joints, the heart, and the nervous system. I guess this possibility is more prevalent in rural areas - a drawback of living in a beautiful part of the country surrounded by fields of sheep. If the sheep are dipped, the ticks look for other hosts to satisfy their lust for blood. It seems as if no-one is exempt, not even folk heros.

While the ticks were heartily devouring William, up in Dumferline a five-year-old black Labrador, called Oscar, was gaily gobbling golf balls. This came to light when his stomach started to rattle! After surgery performed by an astonished local vet, thirteen golf balls were removed from the hapless hound (surely a record haul). Fortunately the fairway thief made a full recovery, but is now more than firmly muzzled during his walks on the local golf course.

I left my tick-free friend at Springfield Kennels, while I presented a Male Continence and Erectile Dysfunction Masterclass in Estoril to 42 English-speaking Portuguese physiotherapists, who had come from all parts of the country. I arrived in rather a mess. My cheeks were hopelessly tear-stained after reading *Rescuing Sprite* by Mark Levin on the plane, a most absorbing book about a rescue dog who touched the family's heartstrings as a youngster and then tugged at them even more while suffering from the effects of a terminal tumour. I didn't know the dog, but I could empathise with Mark's anguish as Sprite became steadily weaker and weaker.

From Lisbon, I flew direct to Dublin where I was met by Nick, who kindly drove me to Kilkenny to present another Male Continence and Erectile Dysfunction Study Day, this time to a lovely group of Irish nurses. We stayed at The Springhill Court Hotel Conference Leisure and Spa Hotel in a room where the radiator behaved during the day but boiled us alive at night.

The next day I shivered, so we visited the exquisite Art and Design Centre in Kilkenny in search of a jumper, but, like all good shopping expeditions, came out with a hat and gloves! Eventually we found some cosy knitwear and headed for Wineport Lodge in Glasson, close to Athlone. We stayed in a suite called 'Burgundy' overlooking a breathtaking lake, where on a former visit, we had seen a beautiful pair of swans protecting a dozen day-old cygnets, which we feared would decrease in number at each morning roll call. The hotel had doubled its size since our last visit and had lost its nautical theme to become a very smart and chic place to stay. We enjoyed it immensely. Not in keeping with its upmarket image was an eclectic model cat collection which cluttered the window sill of the corridor leading to the stylish, new part of the hotel. Each time I walked down the corridor, I moved one of the cats into a compromising position; each day, they were dusted and replaced in their new pose until, at the end of our stay, there was a plethora of passion-crazed pussies.

I left the cats copulating happily (I guess), but wondered if I was going too far in extending everybody's right to a fulfilling sexual relationship to a collection of model cats! From Glasson I headed back to Dublin airport for a flight to Bristol, followed by a drive to Barnstaple where 66 emails were waiting for a reply; four of them were from Channel 4 producers and one concerned an invitation for a book signing (with William) at W.H.Smith in Barnstaple.

The house seemed empty and unloved without William. I missed him. I was going to Finland to teach two days later, so I had decided to leave Wills at the kennels rather than cause him further disruption. During this time, I was able to leave items on the kitchen table and working surfaces with gay abandon and leave the door open with impunity without fear of my best-beloved tearing my belongings to an array of ragged ribbons. Nick felt this was a retrograde step as it would jeopardise all the training that I had undergone, when I had learned (the hard way) to keep everything away from my attack hound.

CHAPTER 11

DOG STAR

WILLIAM STAYED at Springfield Kennels while I was in Finland. I flew from Bristol Airport and changed planes in Paris where I walked a mile (more like ten) from Terminal B to Terminal E. On board, I read 'My Life with George', an inspirational book written by Judith Summers, a young widow, who tried to cheer up her eight-year-old son by taking in a Cavalier King Charles Spaniel for company. George, the Spaniel, was a gifted organiser, who soon had the family pandering to his every royal whim - all except the cat, who never took too kindly to the new resident and became incontinent on the furniture; indeed, with feline cunning, she allowed the new arrival to take the blame! George was either loved or merely tolerated by Judith's potential partners, and always displayed a jealous streak when any new man came into his mistress's life. This book reduced me to tears, so when we touched down, I was a sniffing, snivelling wreck. Not a good way to arrive in Finland!

In Helsinki, I presented Male and Female Continence and Sexual Dysfunction Masterclasses to 24 delightful Finnish physiotherapists who all spoke impeccable English, making me feel very humble for my lack of mastery in a second language. I was booked into a luxury hotel in Helsinki that had been recently converted from a 19th Century prison. It gave me the creeps. That night, when the door clanked shut, I lay in my cell staring at the unforgiving high windows and contemplated how a prisoner would have felt. If I had been guilty of a heinous crime, I imagined I would go mad reliving the felony, until I was riddled with remorse. If I had been wrongly convicted, I would have gone completely bonkers with the total injustice that humanity had inflicted on me, an innocent person. The next day, I was shown one of the original cells with its hard bed, crust of bread,

jug of water and an inbuilt hole for bodily waste; and those for-
bidding high windows bringing in shafts of daylight, which
must have teased and taunted the inmates.

As I was placed in a smoking cell, I asked the janitor if I could
be moved to a non-smoking room. This was not possible for the
first night, as the prison was full of fellow felons. The next day,
I moved rooms and was also handed a black-and-white hori-
zontally-striped T-shirt with my prison number stamped on it.
Great! I was now to be dressed as a convict! "Been to Helsinki
prison, got the T-shirt" was unlikely to impress anyone! While I
was serving my time, I thought about William in his cage. He
had four runs a day in a large field; he exercised in a large field
with the big dog rat-pack; he was combed and cosseted like a
King. It was more Holiday Camp than penitentiary, and all this
while enjoying two scrumptious meals a day with abundantly
more fun than he found at home. I put William to the back of
my mind while I contemplated my own release.

On the flight back, I landed in Paris and, joy of joys, found an
inter-terminal bus to take me swiftly across to Terminal B, which
allowed more time for airport shopping for my grand-daughters. I then stayed the night in a hotel in Bristol before supervis-
ing Christine, my PhD student at The University of the West of
England. The next day I was eager to collect William from
Springfield after a lengthy three weeks, the longest that we had
ever been apart. John and Linda had enjoyed my 'Just William'
book but wanted me to know that their surname was Wharf not
Chalk and that the red-setter mentioned was named Fin (short
for Finbar) not Jip. Suitably apologetic and rightly embarrassed,
I quickly changed the subject to ask how William had behaved.
The report I received was glowing; he had been well-mannered,
had played happily with the other big dogs and, surprisingly,
had not mounted any unsuspecting mutts. Maybe this was
because his mentor, Murphy, was not there! In short, they
thought he was turning into an obedient dog. On arriving home,
he was a delight; he followed me around wagging his tail
happily and seemed pleased to be home at last. We were insep-
arable again.

In preparation for the first book signing I visited a doggy
grooming salon called Hair 'Off' The Dog at the local Pottington
Trading Estate, to request an appointment for William's annual
wash and fluff up. I was turned away as I was not a regular cus-

tomer, and even for the regulars, the stylist was fully booked for the next month. I explained about William's important book signing but this did nothing to achieve a change of heart.

I took my not-so-silky, well-behaved dog to Trelawney Garden Centre for the said book signing, where I attached his lead firmly to my chair and sat down to anchor my excited pet. Glennis joined me with her camera in case my monster played havoc in the store; she was not going to miss this possible fun-filled opportunity for anything! Instead, Wills became the focus of attention for the many locals who flocked through the door (mostly to have lunch on a wet Saturday) though, staggeringly, some eager beavers were buying Christmas cards, paper and decorations in early October!

There were two types of customer: those who delighted in stroking William and those who did not. Those who disliked dogs distanced themselves determinedly. The 'strokers' all reported that they had a dog at home. I learned their dog's names, their misdemeanours and their life stories; indeed, it seemed that many of their dogs were so elderly that they would not last the night. William was a particular success with little children who touched his fur, patted him, cuddled him and many wanted to take him home. What a change from a year ago; then, he would have removed the dummy from the toddler's mouth, run off with all the walking sticks (there were many) and ended up sitting in the rather large push-chair with the twins! I was proud, very proud of my pal, even if his massive attraction meant that I signed only six books in three hours!

The next book signing was scheduled a week later, this time for just an hour, at W.H.Smith in Barnstaple. William was invited too. Glennis was at a dog show that day so was unable to provide any help. I hoped that William would be just as well-mannered now that he had got the hang of it and was a book-signing pro.

While waiting for this prestigious book signing, I was invited by Ann from Trelawney Garden Centre to sign books again on the day that Father Christmas was visiting the store. I guess the main attraction was not me or my books but William, who was extraordinarily good with the children and was fast becoming a beloved pat-a-dog. I told Wills that Santa would probably give him a bone and he readily agreed to attend.

CHAPTER 12

DESTRUCTIVE DAISY

MY GOOD FRIEND Dorothy came down from Surrey to Devon for my birthday, courtesy of Sat Nav. She came via Shrewsbury - but that was scheduled. She brought Daisy, her beautiful eight-year-old pale Golden Retriever, who immediately bonded with William; indeed, I thought that they would fuse together. I was staggered when Dorothy brought the biggest, most expensive, de luxe bed into the kitchen for Daisy, making William's square piece of green, washable matting look rather miserable and a tad spartan. That evening, we went to the Chichester Arms by taxi for a delicious pub supper, so that we could enjoy a bottle of Chilean Merlot together. On our return, the camaraderie took a nose-dive when we found the kitchen covered, absolutely covered, in lumps of white fluffy kapok; Daisy and William had shredded the padded mattress from her vast luxury bed with no thought for her future comfort. We threw the dogs out into the night and laughed helplessly as we stuffed a black dustbin-sack full with the mountains of padding.

Daisy, apparently, normally distanced herself from other dogs, so Dorothy was amazed and delighted by her newfound friendship with William. They slept cuddled together in the king-size, now mattress-free, bed – who needs creature comforts when one is in love? I took my guests to Saunton Sands (Daisy nibbled William's car mat!), where they ran fast and furiously shoulder-to-shoulder as a pack of two, ignoring the other dogs but both preferring to keep out of the water and keen to avoid even the smallest wave.

That evening we met my son, Martin, my daughter-in-law, Jo, and my grand-daughters, Maggie and Charlie, for dinner at The Boathouse in Instow to celebrate my advancing years. Maggie aged five years gave me a birthday card that she had cleverly made herself with a drawing of a cute dog on the front;

inside there were one hundred kisses as she did not know my age and wanted to be sure! Martin and Jo thoughtfully gave me a National Trust subscription, so that I could park free in any of the N.T. car parks when I was out walking with William.

The next night, although I was having a break from cooking (mostly because I felt inferior to Dorothy's superior culinary skills), we decided to eat in, so we bought a lasagne from M&S and, while it was cooking, we relaxed over a glass or two of wine. Dorothy was keen that I should heat up the food correctly: "Was I using the oven and not the microwave? Had I removed the cardboard sleeve? Had I taken off the plastic film?" she plaintively asked. I ignored these unnecessary comments as I laughingly prepared supper.

After twenty minutes, I went into the kitchen to pop some garlic bread into the oven and screamed "Dorothy!". The dogs had ripped one of my cushions to pieces, and the kitchen was knee-high in creamy-white feathers; every working surface was white as were the perpetrators, who produced an effect that movie producers would die for, when they require a swirling snow-storm or blinding blizzard. It seemed impossible that the million wisps of down had escaped from just one cushion; my home resembled a pheasant plucking factory. The delighted dogs ran rings round the kitchen table fluffing up a frenzy of feathers.

I screamed "Dorothy!" repeatedly, but she insisted on finishing the crossword before coming, no doubt knowing what scene of devastation she would find. The feathery-white dogs in duck's clothing were bundled out into the garden, while we stuffed yet another black plastic-sack. I must say I did not laugh as loudly this time but Dorothy was beside herself: "It's not so funny, when it's your cushion, is it?" she laughed. I removed the remaining cushions from the chairs, vacuumed the floor and served a delicious dinner.

This scene should have been a photo opportunity, but we were too appalled by the mess to think 'camera' – indeed neither of us would have been able to hold the lens steady! For ages afterwards, feathers kept appearing from places they had no right to be, as a gentle reminder that the storm had passed, but could re-appear at any time.

Next day we visited the local pet shop, where Dorothy, mindful of Daisy's future comfort, spent £9 on a new matching mattress for her bed, but as her playful hound sat in the car ready to go home, she already started to rip the new purchase to pieces. It was then that Dorothy admitted that Daisy had also ruined her previous bed! After our guests had departed, William sulked all the next day as 'Destructive Daisy' had been the best friend any dog could have; she was beautiful, lively and above all, fun. Just like her owner.

During Dorothy's visit the builders were undertaking reconstruction work on the barn. I wished to make my office, which was next to my bedroom, into an en suite bathroom while my new office would be constructed from an empty loft space in the barn. The building foreman, Reg, was accompanied by a delightful liver-and-white Springer Spaniel, with the now popular name of Marley, who followed him everywhere. Before Daisy arrived, William and Marley played well together, but as soon as the delectable Daisy arrived, Marley was sadly sidelined. Reg told me that his Springer would jump over my five-bar gate, if he went to the other side of the gate and whistled. "Please don't let William see!" I begged. "It will give him ideas....".

Reg and his mate, Craig, set to work digging mounds of earth and rubble out of the barn (as if searching for elusive gold sovereigns) in preparation for lowering the floor and gaining much needed ceiling height. William played happily with Marley until they started digging the drains for a new bathroom to be constructed on the ground floor. I saw the muddy trench and the mountain of earth produced, and knowing Wills's love of mud, decided to keep a close watch every time he ventured outside. I didn't want to take a mucky pup with me to his important book signing.

I took my pristine fluffed and brushed overgrown puppy to W.H.Smith in Barnstaple (actually, he tugged me there!) and anchored his lead to my chair. I sat down firmly and realised that I had forgotten the most important part of a book signer's equipment - my pen! I borrowed a very smart silver pen from John, the manager, while he watched William rearrange the birthday cards with a swish of his tail! William then settled down to meet his adoring public. He was an instant attraction for all the many dog-lovers; he warmed heartily to the attention heaped on him by customers of all ages, while I listened to everyone's tales of woe about their own mischievous and misguided dogs. I learned that one male Golden Retriever slept on his back with all four legs in the air and his mouth hanging open! More 'dead lion' than dog! I signed twelve books in an hour-and-a-half, which was a great improvement on the previous signing (a personal best); I was also asked to sign all the books that were piled on the table for future use. I was happy to oblige. William and I left feeling elated; we had worked as a team now that we had experience; he pulled in the punters, while I sold the books!

My next trip was up to the University of Aberdeen for a meeting about the government-funded trial exploring the effectiveness of pelvic floor exercises for men after prostate surgery. I left William at Springfield Kennels and departed for Bristol, where I stayed close to the airport in The Hilton Hotel for the night, before getting an early plane to Scotland the next day. That evening on the local TV station, I saw a news item showing Sir Michael Parkinson in Taunton signing his new autobiography, *Parky*. There was a long queue of eager people – and without a pretty dog to lure in the customers. I don't mind admitting I was jealous! William would have been furious!

I bought a copy of this popular book at the airport and found it to be so totally fascinating, particularly the early portrayal of the poverty and anguish that surrounded his family of miners, that I was sorry when we touched down. Later that day, I was pleased to climb aboard the plane for the return journey, so that I could continue to read this illuminating story of a thoroughly delightful, humorous, and self-effacing man. He is a man who has met many celebrities - but to Parky the sign of a good person is not their superstar status (unless they have played cricket for Yorkshire), but whether they are a thoroughly nice human being. They win extra points if they make him giggle!

With a heavy heart, I told Steven, my publisher, about Parky's impressive book-signing, but he re-assured me by saying: "It's good to sell twelve books; some authors sit sadly beside their books without anyone asking for a signature!". He also disclosed that 300 copies of *Barking Mad in Barnstaple* had been sold already, even before shoppers had been swept up in the Christmas shopping bonanza. I came off the 'phone and bought William a celebratory present of a marrow-filled bone. He may not be famous (yet), but he was a thoroughly nice chap, who enhanced my life and whom I was privileged to be able to call my best friend (and he made me laugh!). I remembered the mounds of kapok and the swirling feathers filling my kitchen and grinned until my mouth reached beyond my ears.

CHAPTER 13

WILLS THE BUILDER

WILLIAM WAS prepared not just to be a good host to Marley; he wished to be at the centre of the barn conversion works. He wanted to be a master builder. I could tell this was true, because each morning at 8am sharp he helped himself to their equipment; he stole ear-defenders, face-masks, rubber gloves, knee-pads and even ran off with the dust-pan and brush (twice). Reg could not leave the side door of his van open or the hatch-back up for a minute, unless he wanted it emptied by the new, frightfully willing, untrained, unpaid helper. On the negative side, Wills was unable to mix concrete with the same expertise that he had used to whisk feathers; on the positive side, he lived on the site so was quite handy.

Reg and Craig were particularly good keeping the pile of sand covered and out of sight from the resident beach-comber. They covered the drainage trenches and hid pipe-work away from William's prying eyes, but he was sharper than sand and faster than the departing rat that had startled Martin when he was clearing out this part of the barn. Each morning Wills went to work and each morning he was not needed; it was more humiliation than a willing worker could take, so he chewed anything and everything, mostly out of pent up frustration – or just because it was there!

Marley, on the other hand, was an almost perfect six-year-old dog; a non-chewing type (maybe he had no teeth) who just wanted to be close to his master. He would have attained complete perfection if he had taught William exactly how to behave on a building-site, but his teaching skills were sadly lacking - one could say, non-existent.

I needed to vacate a room in the barn for the next stage of

the development. It was amazing how empty rooms had become filled with junk; I had ten years worth of tat that no-one in the family wanted, but that was too good to throw away. Anything that had lain around, unused, for a decade, I deemed superfluous to my requirements. I made three piles: to throw, to charity, and to the loft.

I asked Barry, my gardener, to help me move some of my daughter Claire's belongings, my father's artwork, and Auntie Freda's watercolours up into the loft. He was delighted to help as it was decidedly wet outside with gale-force winds; it seemed preferable to strimming the nettles and brambles, which threatened to enclose my garden. I had just had a concertina loft ladder fitted, but, alas, the pole was too short for me to reach the loop to pull it down. I asked the firm to send me a longer pole, so they kindly sent one that was a foot shorter!

Barry pulled down the ladder, which unfolded effortlessly, took a torch and entered the loft where he reported some tell-tale mice droppings. I leapt up the ladder to inspect the excrement and found it led to a little furry nest. If only I could have persuaded William to report for duty, he could have rounded up the vermin and used his well-honed pouncing skills to exterminate them, but, alas, although he aspired to be a builder, he was not into climbing ladders; he would have to wait for the mice to find him.

I went to St John's Garden Centre to purchase some mouse-killer and found a very smart little box that contained enough of the substance to kill 24 mice. Hoping that I had fewer than 24 unwelcome visitors, I purchased just one box then meekly asked Barry to kindly pop it up in the loft for me.

While I was playing the role of pest-control officer, I visited the vet and purchased an anti-worm tablet and some more anti-tick capsules for Wills. For the benefit of having my dog worm-free for three months and tick-free for six months, I shelled out an amazing £49.50. Worms and ticks, it seems, are expensive pests to eradicate, whereas a mice-free loft would cost only £3.49 or 15 pence per rodent – a bargain if it was effective, provided I had less than 25 furry friends. It seemed that someone was profiteering from parasites, and it wasn't the worms, ticks and mice!

I snuck the gigantic yellow pill, designed to knock all

worms on the head, into a similarly-coloured piece of cheese by designing a neat slot and burying the tablet within. Now William may eat like a wolf, but he cleverly ate the cheese and spat out the pill, which cost a mammoth £8.68, onto the floor. Round one to Wills, followed by rounds two and three. I then admitted resounding defeat and gave up. I went round Tescos looking for something in which to conceal the drug and left with a chicken cordon bleu breast for us to share. I would add vegetables to my meal while Wills would have a garlic-scented pill in a pocket. I then asked Glennis how she coped with all her dogs. "Easy," she replied. "Just grind the tablet up between two spoons and sprinkle it onto his meal. And it's much cheaper if you buy it on the web!" Thus William devoured a delicious three-layered breakfast with a dried dog-food base, a powdered pill surprise, topped off with a tasty raw egg. Possibly just the kind of meal that discerning worms prefer!

Martin and family popped in to view the restoration project. What had started with enthusiasm had slowly ground to a standstill waiting for the Building Inspector's approval (Oh! and the workmen were all needed on Monday morning when a mega-load of ready-mix cement was being delivered to another site, where they needed the full work-force to spread the load over, presumably, the length and breadth of Devon).

Martin mentioned that my building project reminded him of his Grandpop, my dear father, who was happiest working with wood. Hence his garden in Totteridge had grown a shed at each corner until semi-detached sheds started to appear and threatened to merge with the chicken-run. When he retired and moved to Dorset, my mother limited this ardent shed-proliferator to a large workshop, where he taught carpentry skills to his six young grandchildren, who were each given their own tool-box and who learned, under his skilled guidance, the rudiments of sawing, hammering and screwing, while standing on a box! He was a born teacher, so all the grandsons and granddaughters grew up with honed practical skills passed down from the long 'Blundell' line of carpenters, shop-front fitters and coffin makers.

While Martin was there, I proudly showed him my new loft ladder, mainly for him to count how many mice had lost the will to live. Disappointingly, no mouse was lying on its back with its legs in the air - not one. Had they all skipped ship? Were they super-mice who were resistant to this cheap product? Did I need a military-sized killing kit? As I was musing, Maggie and Charlie nimbly climbed up the ladder to investigate the problem, expecting to find some cute furry animals. They assured me that my loft was now mouse-free, but please could they have Auntie Claire's teddy!

Martin's family had arrived in a camper van with Bob the puppy, who was a poor traveller. I had forgotten, in just a few short months, how inconveniently puppies behave; Bob had thrown up in the van, leaked urine with sheer excitement in the kitchen and gone absolutely wild, verging on mental, when he met William. The two dogs romped around together, rolling into an eight-legged ball. Each game ended with a dominant William pressing a large paw firmly on top of Bob, who rolled onto his back in full submission; at one time Wills opened his mouth to engulf Bob's head completely and still Bob wanted more. I thought they would joust to the death. Once his energetic rival had gone, Wills collapsed on the kitchen floor looking lifeless and legless. Puppies were exhausting!

The next day I was scheduled to stay with Maggie and Charlie while Martin and Jo had a break and enjoyed Sunday lunch (a school raffle prize) at a restaurant in Parkham. I left Wills at home as I thought it would be mayhem looking after two energetic grandchildren and two hyperactive dogs. All went well until Charlie went into the conservatory and shut the sliding glass door. It stuck! Charlie was unable to open it from outside and I could not move it from inside. I now had one granddaughter shut in the conservatory and one with me in the lounge plus Bob, who was unable to reach the garden for a pee. I panicked and telephoned Martin, who cleverly had turned his mobile off. We were on our own.

Maggie came up with the solution: we should go out through the front door to reach Charlie. Why does anxiety prevent rational thought? Obviously in an emergency situation, I needed to be led by a child of five. I went round the house and, with one enormous tug, I was able to open the glass door and restore Bob's exit route and, along with it, my sanity.

The last time I had door trouble was when Glennis asked me to let her six Golden Retrievers out into the garden while she was out. I arrived, unlocked the house and stared at the child-proof gate, which confined the dogs to the kitchen. I pulled, squeezed and shoved every part of the gate and was totally unable to open it. Maggie would have known what to do! I have to admit I gave up the struggle, admitted defeat, found a chair and climbed over into a kitchen filled with quizzical dogs. After doing my good deed, I had to conduct another obstacle manoeuvre to arrive back onto the chair.

The next time I was invited to let the dogs out, I found that the child-gate had been thoughtfully left open with just the door to the kitchen shut. This meant that my entrance and exit should have been easy. I sussed how I had to squeeze one bit of plastic while lifting another and felt mightily pleased with myself. But on my departure, as I was shutting the gate, I put one leg out to confine one of the dogs, then needed the other leg to stop another dog from leaving while a third intrepid monster escaped between my legs!

CHAPTER 14

PAT-A-DOG

MINDFUL OF THE pleasure that William had given to children and adults alike at the book signings, I decided to telephone North Devon Adult Hospice and The Children's Hospice to see if they would like a visit from a physiotherapist with a friendly Golden Retriever. My idea was to help cheer up patients who would benefit from having a dog to stroke. Physiotherapists are experienced in finding the correct words to say to help patients who are unwell, and I liked the idea of using my physiotherapeutic knowledge to enhance the lives of some of the terminally ill patients. I also wanted to do something in return for all the wonderful care that Maggie had experienced when she suffered from leukaemia as a one-year-old toddler.

I telephoned The Children's Hospice first and was told that someone would get back to me. I then rang the Adult Hospice to find that a lady with a dachshund (this sounded like my friend, Judith, from the tennis club) had volunteered the previous week to help, but that they would keep my name on file. The Manager told me: "We allow pets to visit here, so there would be very few instances when we may need you." He thanked me for my interest and I felt that I would not hear from him again.

I left my un-patted dog at Towsers Kennels while I was away for a mixture of business and pleasure. I always felt guilty leaving him, so I gently explained to William that if he wanted me to keep him in delicious puppy nuts and treats, I had to earn some respectable money. He looked at me incredulously and rushed into the kennels to party. The guilt I felt was akin to the guilt I felt when I ran a physiotherapy practice from home in Chesham Bois. My daughter Claire announced one day: "You think more of your patients than you do of us!" I gently replied that I was trying to provide for their holidays abroad and save up for both of them to have a car when they were seventeen (no motor bikes - I broke my leg on the back of one when I was sixteen). My son Martin would use the situation to his advantage by posting me notes, including his school report, under the clinic door and then making a run for it! Eventually, many happy patients later, Claire had a blue 2CV costing £2000 (the cheapest new car on the road) and the next year Martin had a red one.

Eventually Claire's car needed upgrading so my dear father kindly bought her a newer model resplendent in green and cream. When she went to live in Hong Kong, she parked it on the front lawn of our house in The Fennings. Then Martin's car broke down before a trip to Devon to celebrate his 30th birthday, and he telephoned Claire to see if he could borrow her car. He received no reply, so he rather unwisely decided to give her car a trip to the South West.

I then received a frantic series of calls from Martin at BUPA Hospital Bushey, where I was Physiotherapy Manager. As I was collected from working on the wards, the receptionist relayed the messages to me. "Please could I speak to Mrs Dorey?" Martin had asked, then "Please could I speak to Grace Dorey?" followed swiftly by a third call requesting: "Please can I speak to my mummy?", "This call sounds expensive!" I murmured.

Martin had been leaving the M5 when he felt his feet becoming hot, then he was horrified to see flames appearing round his ankles! He stopped on the roundabout, ripped off his seat belt and ran. He looked back to see the car exploding in a ball of flames. This left him not only horribly shocked, but in the difficult situation of how, just how, could he tell his sister. How? We telephoned Claire in Hong Kong and quite understandably she was not a happy bunny, more like a hopping-mad March hare. "I wanted to keep my car forever, in memory of my Grandpop," she cried. To compound the problem, her insurance only covered 'third party' and not 'fire and theft'.

The conflict was not helped when Martin tactlessly bought her a birthday card with a photograph of a 2CV on the front and burnt it all the way round with a cigarette! This tense situation was only remedied when I gave Claire the money to purchase another car, thus avoiding sibling niggling and restoring family unity.

Once again I paid my way out of trouble by leaving William at Towsers Kennels. The owner, Sue, asked for my email address so that she could send me some photographs that she had taken of my 'handsome William' when he was a puppy. She assuaged my guilt by saying how much she loved him. I thanked her, then drove up to Birmingham for my debut on the Channel 4 programme 'Embarrassing Illnesses'. I was worried that I might be the one displaying embarrassment, as I was sure to blush pillar-box-red, but that day the weather was freezing the tits off the trees so, despite wearing a T-shirt as a vest, I quickly became a delicate shade of blue. I stood on a stage between the two good-looking doctors, Pixie and Christian, who were both exceptionally tall and slim, feeling more like a frosted mushroom than a TV star. Rain threatened, the wind swept in from the North Pole and became icier by the second, so despite copious cajoling from the camera crew, we all agreed to do it in one take. We were, after all, medical professionals not film stars!

While I was waiting for filming to commence, I was interviewed by the local Midlands BBC Radio station. The presenter identified with the problem that many women face, as she herself had experienced the shock and embarrassment of trampoline-induced leakage. She asked me the best way to activate the pelvic floor muscles and, more importantly, during which particular activities. A helicopter circled overhead, possibly taking shots of the assembled crowd, but the incessant droning noise of the blades only served to delay filming. By this time I was frozen to the bone and only dreamed of sitting in front of a roaring fire with a mug of hot chocolate!

My role was to teach the people of Birmingham the correct way to perform pelvic floor muscle exercises. I had never seen this before on television, so welcomed the idea of teaching men, women and children 'how' and, even more importantly, 'when' to tighten their pelvic floor muscles. The producer wanted me to stand on a trampoline holding a megaphone, which was something that I instantly declined to do! A shot of me with my legs in the air was not exactly the image that I wished to portray to viewers at home and would also have been frowned upon by the Chartered Society of Physiotherapy.

Instead, I held a microphone and faced a blurry University Rugby team (vanity insisted that I removed my glasses!), whom I was unable to see, but could certainly smell! They were wearing rank kit that had lain unwashed for three weeks. I set to work. The testosterone-charged rugger team were taught to tense their undercarriage strongly while chanting. In contrast, I also taught some beautiful young, intensely-energetic cheer-leaders to tighten their pelvic floor muscles to the music 'Can You Feel It?' by The Jacksons. Importantly, the girls were taught to clench their muscles strongly during coughing, sneezing, singing, shouting, lifting and even during sexual activity. They were taught to walk around Birmingham with their heads held high with a slight lift of their pelvic floor providing a visual illus-tration of perfect posture.

After the performance, Pixie and Christian jumped off the stage and quickly disappeared into the warm 45 foot-long trailer, leaving little me shivering on the platform waiting to be helped down by one of the many crew. I left Birmingham (and my lovely mohair hat that Nick had kindly given me) wondering how much footage would finish on the cutting-room floor by March 2009, when the programme was due to be broadcast. I hoped and expected that they would quickly ditch those close-up shots that they had captured when one over-zealous cam-eraman had held a lens the size of a square dinner-plate up to my nose (I would have welcomed it 40 years ago, but not now!). Much later, I learned that the sound recording was not good, so Channel 4 had decided not to broadcast my part! Perhaps I should have welcomed the megaphone a little more readily! I then headed for the M6 and M1 where I battled through the Friday night traffic to reach my good friend Judy in St Albans, who was waiting with warm welcome and a compulsory glass of wine.

The next day we had planned to visit Eileen, a friend of ours with Multiple Sclerosis, who had been an excellent Physiother-apy Receptionist at West Herts Hospital in Hemel Hempstead many moons ago, when Judy and I were young physiothera-pists eager to advance our careers. Eileen was one of those special people in whom we were able to confide, and who delighted in our good fortune and empathised with our many (too many) moans. We found Eileen in a motorised wheelchair able only to move her left arm. She was renting a flat in a Private Care Home, where she had a hoist fixed over her bed and a fully-equipped, disabled kitchen and new wet room that she, herself, had purchased.

I shuddered when I heard that every time Eileen wanted help to get in or out of bed, she had not only to wait for one of the all too few carers, but she had to pay for the privilege; even then, she always got up later and went to bed earlier than she would have wished. Eileen reported that, despite her ambulatory problems, she had full bladder control. However, it cost £16.50 every time she needed help to use the lavatory. I was appalled; this situation could lead to cutting down on fluids with serious urological consequences.

I gave Eileen a copy of *Barking Mad in Barnstaple* which she was delighted to receive saying: "I can read this when I have to go to bed early". My own worries seemed vacuous and trite compared to the restrictions that Eileen had to bear on a daily basis. Despite the vast difficulties she was facing, she was so outgoing, full of fun and, as always, a joy and delight to be with. An unsung brave bunny – no wonder my eyes started to fill up with tears.

Over a delicious lunch that Judy had kindly provided, Eileen confided that her daughter Lyn, aged 40, had just been diagnosed with Acute Progressive Multiple Sclerosis, the same strain as her mother, for which there was no cure at the present time. I left in tears. How could life be so appallingly cruel.

From St Albans, I met the physiotherapists with whom I trained at The Royal London Hospital for our annual reunion, a mammoth 46 years since we left. Fourteen of us, including some brave husbands, met for lunch at The Nag's Head at Great Missenden. Everyone wanted to purchase a signed 'William' book after I disclosed that I had written about last year's reunion. Janine and Gill laughed helplessly as I read the account of her fateful Mad-Hatter's tea-party during William's wantonly destructive phase. I guess if you want to sell books, you tell the customers that they are mentioned in it - which must be why *Who's Who?* does so well.

We all agreed that next year, when it would be 50 years since we first met as fellow students, we should celebrate in style with dinner and a night in a hotel. I was charged with finding a suitable venue somewhere in the Cotswolds for this golden occasion and giving everyone sufficient notice of the date (most of the set were not working, but had social calendars crammed full of exciting activities).

I left St Albans for Cheltenham, where I was presenting a

'Female Continence and Sexual Dysfunction Study Day' to physiotherapists, in good time in order to break my journey at Cribbs Causeway for a little mooch round John Lewis. In the shop, I spied some white crease-resistant cotton sheets that would be ideal for my new guest bedroom (as yet un-constructed). The price was reduced by 20%, so I bought a set (for a bed that I have not yet bought!). It was only as I was walking through the shopping mall, that I realized that I had been in M&S and not John Lewis!

I consoled myself in the store that I had come to visit by stroking the fur hats in the hat department; most were faux fur and failed to satisfy my fetish, but there was one little number that was wonderfully-fluffy sheepskin; I tried it on, liked what I saw (except for the price) and determinedly walked away. I was drawn back twice to try the hat on again, all the while convincing myself that it would not be there next time I was in Bristol. Finally, I meekly gave in and bought it. Now that the days were drawing in and the temperature was dropping, I considered that this impulsive purchase would be wonderfully cosy when walking through blizzards and worse with Wills. Nick had invited William and me (in that order!) to France for two weeks over Christmas and the New Year, so I could wear my beautiful bonnet on the blustery beaches of Brittany! What better justification!

The next day I rushed to collect William from Towsers, paid for his holiday, made a huge fuss of him, and let him jump into the boot of the car - unlike one dizzy customer who came to collect her dog, paid the kennel and forgot to take him home! I may not know which shop I am in, I may find fur utterly irresistible, but at least I remembered to leave the kennels with a dog!

CHAPTER 15

TAMING BOB

MARTIN TELEPHONED to discuss Bob's problems. There were many. Mainly, he was a poor traveller and threw up at every opportunity. Then he developed kennel cough coupled with bouts of unpleasant vomiting, a condition that he possibly passed on to the rest of the class at 'Puppy Gurus'. Sadly, he was unable to attend the last training day, when all the clever puppies were invited to perform a trick. He had been practising a routine where he rushed across the room and leapt high into the air before landing on Charlie's red beanbag with a thud, but he was spared from displaying such a riveting performance by the vet. He was grounded.

Restricting such a lively puppy as Bob was tricky; he had learned how to escape from his cage through the corner, where the metal panels should meet, and had mastered the art of tugging humans in the direction he preferred to travel. Martin had cured both problems, one with enough rivets to build another Eiffel Tower and the other with a body harness which restricted Bob's front legs and prevented him from flooring any of the family. On reflection, both problems could have been solved simply by riveting the little darling to the floor!

My friend, Sally, had kindly given me a red harness (with silver reflective paw prints) for William when he was a small and wilful puppy, though as it was too large, I had popped it away in a drawer. I decided to try it out again. William thought it was great fun; he kept looking up at me to see if I was still with him and seemed to prefer his new found freedom from having *me* tug his collar. He now had to shorten his stride, so without an ounce of pride and with his tail feathers held high, he wiggled his butt deliciously as he minced down the lane. It certainly stopped the brute from pulling, so I decided to buy him a model in black for Christmas - red was not his colour!

The insurance provider, Petguard, had done some new research into people's choice of dog in different regions of the country. They found that people in the South West were more likely to have a Golden Retriever, those living in Wales chose Labradors, those in London predominantly selected Pugs, while in Yorkshire it was no surprise to find that most folk preferred Yorkshire terriers. The next question had to be why Devon was over-run with Goldies? Had Glennis and her fellow breeders populated this fine county with William's relatives, or could it have been that only those with a cherished pedigree dog could afford to (or afford not to) insure their pet and therefore skewed this piece of research? Surely more people own cross-breeds than expensive pedigree dogs? What about the dogs with M&S insurance like William? Had Wills been counted at all? Had they considered the possibility that people sub-consciously choose dogs that looked like themselves?

It is possible that people gradually become more like their pet in the way that elderly couples look more like brother and sister with the passage of time. I decided to scrutinize my fellow dog-walkers for similarities to their pets. Bob certainly did not look like any of Martin's family, though if my son grew a beard again and dyed it black, I would have to rethink.

This 'part Terrier, part Springer' was waltzing to his own tune: he could sit to order and come when called, but last thing at night, when he was let out into the garden, he refused to come back inside. He went on the prowl and became a creature of the night, a veritable stop-out. It was at this stage in William's development that I started taking him out on the lead first thing in the morning and also for a last pee at 7pm (later than that he simply fell asleep and would not walk!). This regime was altogether simpler and less harrowing than waiting, for ever, for him to return. I suggested this to Martin, who, in turn, suggested it to Bob.

I had to leave William again at Towsers holiday camp, so I bundled him in with his mat, comb, toy and more than enough quality dog food for his stay; I bought the best lest they thought I was feeding him junk. Sue said: "You don't need to bring food; we provide it." What a revelation! I had been bringing food with me for two years thinking that the same rules applied as those at Springfield Kennels. Sue had always thought that I had wanted William to have special food! I made a mental note never to provide even a crumb of sustenance when he stayed again, cursed myself for not realizing, while at the same time counted up the number of expensive bags I had bought unnecessarily.

I was scheduled to attend a 20-year anniversary dinner of the Association of Chartered Physiotherapists in Independent Healthcare in London. As I had the honour of being their president, I had prepared a welcome speech for their meeting the next day. I presented a pictorial history of the last 20 years, sneaking in a picture of William as a puppy and then as a fully grown madly handsome dog to illustrate how things increase in size and hopefully make the presentation more entertaining (for dog lovers!). I reflected how the group had grown considerably over a couple of decades. I found photographs of our 10-year anniversary at The House of Lords when Claire Oldroyd was the president and I was the chair; since then I had moved to Devon where my life was centred around two gorgeous grandchildren and, of course, William.

I left my best beloved for one extra day (£9.25 including two hearty meals a day) at Towsers as I had agreed to look after Maggie and Charlie for the night while Martin celebrated his birthday with Jo at the 40th birthday party of another Martin in Reading. I felt that I was totally unable to look after two children and an energetic puppy at Martin's house if William was with me! I popped Bob in his pen, then I took the children to Atlantic Village Shopping Mall, where we met Glennis and her granddaughter, Jordan, so that the children could visit the play area and release a chunk of energy before settling down sedately to watch 'Strictly Come Dancing' with me! While we were out I bought each of them a red velvet dress for Christmas and also a toy; they chose 'High School Musical' dolls and seemed to accept that they would be hidden until Christmas Day.

Bob's antics made me think how far I had come with William. He ran off, at the speed of a laser, with anything that was left on the floor in his mouth, before emptying the shelves to a height of three feet. The more dismayed the children became, the friskier Bob became. You could see that look of superior defiance as he crunched DVDs, dragged cushions twice his size the length of the room and ran away with a selection of shoes. Soon, there was not enough space on the top shelves to put things out of his way. He leapt up and grabbed hold of any flapping clothing that the children were wearing, even though they had learnt to turn their back on the 'monster'. It was a treat to look after the children, but Bob was something different. He reminded me, in a fearful flash, exactly why I would never have another puppy again. Never! He had enough energy to illuminate, and perchance fuse, all the Christmas lights on the planet. But Maggie and Charlie were my stars; they gave their own rendition of 'X Factor' wearing their nightwear, happily performing between me and the television. Later, I bundled these two sleepy people into their bunk beds before persuading Bob to spend the whole night in his cage.

I was woken at 3am by a tearful Maggie who had experienced a nasty nightmare and needed reassurance, so she climbed into bed with me. Before long, Charlie cottoned on to the same ploy, until we were 'three-in-the-bed'. The situation was eased considerably when Maggie asked plaintively: "Please may I go back to my bed?", to which I dozily replied: "Of course, darling". As she closed the door behind her, she said: "I love you, Gran Gran." "I love you too", I replied as she tiptoed to her room.

The next day I took the children to Towsers to collect William and asked Shaun if they could see the dogs in the kennels. We were given a guided tour; William was in the first cage turning cartwheels; the other pens were filled with every breed of dog you could imagine, some recognisable, some not; one of the cages contained two dogs that the children recognised as twins. All the dogs barked as we walked past, but became quiet once we had left. We took William home before rushing back to give Bob a walk.

When Martin and Jo returned, I reported how wonderful the children had been, then cursorily mentioned that I had introduced Maggie and Charlie to Bob's new kennels, explaining just how much he would enjoy making friends with the other dogs (and hoping that I might be spared puppy-sitting). Now that his kennel cough had gone, he could have a droplet of vaccine up one nostril to satisfy the kennel's requirements and Bob's your uncle!

CHAPTER 16

A BOOK FOR CHRISTMAS

ITH THE HELP of Martin as editor, I had written a book titled *Pump Up Your Penis: easy exercises to strengthen your erection*, which I particularly wanted to hit the shelves in time for Christmas. This little hard-backed book contained a cartoon on every other page and aimed to show men, in an amusing way, how and why to perform pelvic floor muscle exercises. While it was of value to all men, I wanted to keep it well away from Wills. The thought of him gaining permission to indulge in some seamless shagging was not on my agenda. He was still a 'complete' male and a virgin, and I wanted to keep it this way. Sadly for William and happily for me, the kennels did not accept bitches in season. Somehow, he had known what to do ever since he was eight weeks old; he took socialisation to a new level at the vet's Puppy Party when he bonked Meg, a dirty Collie bitch. Since that time he has mounted a few (too many!) male dogs.

I was warned at the Puppy Classes that family pets should not be used as studs, as their libido would increase together with their wanderlust. I had to break this gently to his hornyship and upped his pocket money accordingly. I felt a little guilty that, at a professional level, I was encouraging men (and women) to have sexual satisfaction, but denying my dog the opportunity to express his basic animal instincts and his desire to become a swash-buckling sex-god. He had the inclination, the pedigree, the looks, a physique to die for, and stamina galore; he would love to populate the County with little Williams, but could Devon cope? It seemed that the South-West was already awash with Goldies; would he be putting the other studs' noses out-of-joint or, worse still, pushing them out onto the streets?

I undertook another book-signing of *Barking Mad* at Trelawney Garden Centre, where one customer was waiting for me. Having borrowed William's book from Northam Library, she now wished to purchase a copy for her daughter. I sold seven books in an hour-and-a-half; most purchases were for Christmas presents. William was in seventh heaven receiving copious cuddling and cosseting. One lady told me that her elderly mother's puppy was so hyperactive that it was given tranquillizers; when this did nothing to relieve the stressful situation, her mother was prescribed sedatives! I realized then that writing wicked William's story had indeed spared me from becoming a pill-popper.

Glennis popped in to see me at Trelawney with Jordan, who wanted to see Father Christmas and his sleigh, complete with live husky goats (the nearest thing to huskies that Devon could produce) and live reindeer resplendent in pens. Nowadays children can choose which toy they would like, so Jordan chose a baby doll, which was exactly the item that William would have chosen; he made a bee-line for the present. Indeed, if his lead had not been firmly secured to my chair, he would have been the proud owner of crying, squeaking, gurgling infant doll. Glennis kindly took William home for me (though she had trouble persuading him to board her car!) when I was kindly collected by Ruth and Jenny for Sunday lunch at Saunton Sands Golf Club.

This was a wonderful way to spend a blustery day. We sat on a table by the window and enjoyed the panoramic view of an empty golf course; the only vestige of civilisation was a yellow flag, waving its socks off, like the prayer flags flapping feverishly in the gales faraway in mountainous Tibet. Ruth was a member of this prestigious golf club and particularly wanted to treat Jenny (my friend from the tennis club) and myself to an old-fashioned Sunday roast. Jenny told us that she had saved up all year to go on 'the trip of a lifetime' to Antarctica. The lunch was superb, made particularly enjoyable by the entertaining company, but the day disappeared in a twinkling until we realized that it was 3.30pm and Trelawney shut their gates (with my car inside) at 4pm. So the long chatty lunch came to an abrupt end, when we dashed to claim my car before it was gated for the night!

Sadly, exactly three weeks later to the day, dear Jenny Metcalfe had a massive brain bleed when she was on the boat close to Antarctica and needed to be air-lifted to hospital in South Georgia. Tragically, she died without gaining consciousness. Ruth, her long-term friend, and I will miss her energy, vitality and infectious cheerfulness. She was the fittest and youngest of the three of us and thought nothing of horse-riding in the morning and playing tennis in the afternoon. Sometimes, life can be so cruel and devastatingly unfair.

Dave, the wonderful foreman carpenter (and also the brother of my boss, Debbie), has a Jack Russell named Oakley who accompanies him to work. The peace-loving Marley has had problems with Oakley in the past, so I kept William inside when Oakley was tethered on a long lead in the garden, rather than letting the dogs have a scrap. I preferred to take Wills down the lane, rather than have an alfresco free-for-all. One day, we were walking down the lane when, suddenly, I saw two young girls on horse-back, each leading another unsaddled horse. I froze. I had visions of William barking and jumping up at all four horses. I looked for a fence post to secure the lead, but could find nothing suitable at short notice. I asked William to sit, but he was much too interested in these fine animals to obey. Mercifully, he did not pull; he just stared. "He is a puppy." I said, untruthfully, in case they saw the lack of blood in my white knuckles and the abject terror in my eyes. After they passed (thankfully, uneventfully), my hound pulled me back up the hill to the comfort of his home. He knew when he was the underdog.

Later that day, I read in *The Daily Telegraph* that the smallest foal in the world had been born in Melbourne, Australia. It was a silver dun Tovero foal and stood at almost 15 inches, just the size of a week-old lamb. I decided to measure my 'puppy'. When standing, he stood 24 inches high to the top of his back, but an amazing 36 inches to the top on his head. William was larger than a pony; no wonder he was as strong as a horse. I considered buying him a cart for Christmas to attach to his new black harness.

My friend, Judy, came down for a brilliant weekend. The weather was crisp and sunny, so we were able to walk along the length of Saunton Sands beach with William. Judy is one of those people who do not take to dogs; she prefers Pinky, her 40 year-old tortoise, who was busy hibernating in the garage wearing her mother's woollen vest. William is one of those pets who are overly-anxious to impress; he was not used to being ignored. He turned cartwheels, forward-rolls and back-flips in vain. I, of course, was amused by his effort to gain friends, but Judy was unimpressed; she still preferred her Pinky.

On Saturday Mary and Tony joined us for lunch and to see how much my cute little puppy had grown. "Last time we visited you, he was a tiny pup in a large pen over there in the corner of the kitchen," Tony said. They were amazed by his size; he was bigger than Mary's Labrador, Bodger, who was considered to be a giant among dogs and who regularly escaped by jumping clean over the garden gate. Sadly, this behaviour had cost Mary not only a big vet's bill, but their beloved Bodger, his balls.

William was still complete; he had hung onto his testicles, while I hung onto the belief that obedience was the key to all behavioural issues (though I did hope that owners of bitches on heat would keep them inside and save my dog from losing his much-protected virginity).

My virile dog was still getting excited when anyone appeared at my door; he was still barking to announce the arrival of my visitors, but he needed to learn not to jump up and tower over my guests, when he became menacingly ten feet tall; in short, he needed to keep all four feet flat on the floor. How could I curb his excitement? I took to popping him in the car just before guests arrived, so that they entered the house first. This prevented a good deal of pure puppy pleasure, but was welcomed by my guests, who were guarding their beautiful best clothes. If we ate in the kitchen, I gave Wills a liver-filled bone so that he would refrain from pawing my guests' thighs in an attempt to receive a stroke.

It was my behaviour that was changing; I kept the kitchen door to the hall closed, I never ever left food around, I kept all objects away from his clutches. But if I failed, he considered that the object was his as he crunched up anything and everything within reach!

Now that Wills had eaten all the builders' tools and a good deal of their safety equipment, they were more than ready to hand over my new office in the barn. They had cleared an area ready for the delivery of my latest book, *Pump Up Your Penis* but the pallet of twenty boxes failed to arrive. I telephoned the printers who informed me that it was not loaded onto the van. The next day I rushed back from my clinic to await a one o'clock delivery, only to receive a telephone call from the apologetic van driver who had, unfortunately, experienced a puncture in Ilchester. He eventually arrived with four inflated tyres at 6.45pm just as I was leaving to go into Barnstaple.

That day, I had been invited by Waterstone's book shop to do a book signing of *Barking Mad* at 7pm, when the store opened for late-night shopping in the run-up to Christmas. Peter, the deputy Manager, was sorry to let me know that there was no room at the inn for William (they had read the book and were forewarned!), so I left the literary star at home while I signed fifteen books in an hour-and-a-half as his proud author. The manager of Waterstone's was very pleased with the sales to date, as he had now sold 46 books; he even asked me to sign five books as Christmas presents for his staff. I was delighted; out of all the thousands of books in the store, he had chosen mine! William was becoming a local hero.

CHAPTER 17

HAPPY BIRTHDAY WILLS

WILLIAM WAS going to be a big two-year-old on December 5th. In anticipation of this momentous event, I emailed Glennis:

Dear Glennis

I would like to invite both you and Jordan to pop in some-time over the weekend for William's 2nd Birthday Party.

Please bring a suitable friend for William, that he won't dominate or hump. I cannot invite John's bitch, as Wills will ride her all the way home and little Bob would probably land up in the birthday cake.

With love
Grace

On his birthday, I gave William an extra big hug, while I considered how far we had come in the last two years. He was a good-looking, large, loveable dog whom I absolutely adored. William was now, in human terms, fourteen years of age – that was the age when school dominated my life, when I loved sport best, when I lived for ballet lessons, but above all I was more interested in the opposite sex. I can remember, at that age, I made a list of all the boys that I knew from Union Church Youth Club in Totteridge (I knew 100) and decided that I fancied only 5%! William was not that selective, so would continue to need a chaperone – I quickly volunteered.

I alerted my three builders and my gardener to the fact that William may be a wee bit overexcited as it was his second birthday, while they smiled politely and feigned mock interest. They probably would have been more intrigued to know that it was also the 50 year anniversary of the opening of the first stretch of Motorway bypassing Preston, which later became the M6 - or even that 50 years ago to the day, the first long-distance telephone call was made from London to Inverness. As he was short of presents, William helped himself to a large yellow painting-sponge and scattered pieces of it not so neatly over the drive. I felt guilty leaving my friend on his birthday, but Friday was the day when I played indoor tennis, so I gave him a new birthday marrow-bone to enjoy, thereby assuaging my guilt. Chez, Doug, Ray, Roger and Don (all of whom wanted mentioning in my book!) insisted that I took a tennis ball home for him. He walked round the kitchen with the yellow ball in his mouth, with his ears and jowls wider than usual, feeling important, even though he was completely hopeless at catching a ball and even more hopeless at dropping it to order.

On Saturday, Glennis arrived with Jordan at 4pm for William's party. For the birthday boy, it was not the best of celebrations. Unfortunately, no doggy friend arrived, as Glennis's dogs were suffering from a particularly virulent strain of kennel cough, which affected even those dogs who had been vaccinated. The party animal was overjoyed to receive his human guests. In fact, he performed a series of leaps designed to be a choreographed greeting, but served to prevent Glennis and Jordan from opening the five-barred gate. They kindly arrived with a comical card, which had to be placed high on the window-sill out of the William's reach in case it met the same fate as both of my address books, and a long bone, which was very well-received and immediately carried off down the garden in case it was taken away.

Maggie, Charlie and I had made some little birthday cakes earlier that day. I had intended to make a carrot cake, but had found that the flour at the back of my cupboard was plain and not self-raising, and was also out of date! So we made a dozen little chocolate oat cakes (too soggy and far too sweet), even though we knew that William could not have one as dogs are not allowed to have chocolate.

Maggie had been learning about old cottages like mine at school. "When your cottage was built, there was no electricity," she proudly announced. I was impressed with her level of education, until she followed it with: "Gran Gran, were you living here then?". I laughed and somehow still let her scrape out the bowl, while Charlie licked the wooden spoon.

Party-time for William became too exciting; he behaved like a hyperactive child trying to jump up to the table and rearrange the party tea. Sadly and rather ironically, he was relegated to the boot of the car while we celebrated two glorious years of loving William!

CHAPTER 18

A HOLIDAY WISH LIST

I POPPED INTO St John's Veterinary Clinic to have William's chip scanned in preparation for his visit to France; the scanner read his number instantly, reassuring me that he was ready to sail. While I was there, I asked the receptionist if I could weigh my monster, who had his own ideas. He would not walk onto the scales despite repeated cajoling and even an offer of a tasty treat. He was as stubborn as a mule with attitude. In the end, rather than admit that I had a wilfully disobedient dog, I lifted up my feisty hound and plonked him onto the weighing platform - all 35.2 Kilos of him. It was a wonder that he did not break the scales (or my back). Then he sat down and resolutely refused to dismount, no doubt expecting me to carry him home!

I went into St John's Garden Centre to purchase an identity disc so that he could wear his French address on his collar. When we were there last year, the only identification that my escapologist sported was his compulsory shoulder-blade chip and a numerical ear tattoo. Now we were going into over-kill – like sporting a belt, braces *and* truss! If William strayed and was unable to find his way home, he could now be delivered to the villa by any 'gentil Monsieur' who was strong enough to lift him into his vehicle. In any case, I felt reassured!

Nick telephoned and thought it would be better if his mobile 'phone number was written on the identity disc. Martin telephoned to let me know that it was illegal in France to have a dog without identity; apparently unidentified stray dogs could be taken to the pound and destroyed. I shuddered. Martin also told me that Bob had been castrated in order to stop him from humping Maggie and Charlie. This behaviour continued during his convalescent period, so they bought a water spray, which was eminently more effective. However, for Bob, his operation did have one compensation; he could now jump clear over the pet-guard gate and enter the bedrooms without snagging his balls!

I went into the local stores in Landkey to buy a local paper, as it contained a review of *Barking Mad in Barnstaple*, designed to tempt readers to buy copies as Christmas presents for their family and friends. The proprietor told me that a pit bull terrier, which was loose in the village, had attacked a dog walking innocently on a lead, biting through its neck. The badly-injured victim had to be rushed down to the veterinary hospital. The Dog Patrol Officer had been alerted and was trying to round up the attacker before there was another similar incident. I think the aggressive pit bull terrier's days were numbered; indeed, if he was caught, he would either be muzzled for life or possibly put down. Had the terrier been dumped from another area or had he lived locally and escaped? Hopefully the dog had an identity disc so that its owners could be traced and even prosecuted.

While I was at the village shop, I had left William in the car in preparation for a walk on the Green, but after this scare, I turned the car round and headed for home. I feared for his safety and retreated in order to prevent him from being the next unwitting casualty.

Back at home, I received the delivery of a large box from Over The Top pet accessories; it contained a set of black boot covers to protect Nick's new VW Golf from the mud, fur and detritus that dogs regularly deposit in cars by the ton. I was also delighted to find that Nick had kindly ordered me another set of boot covers for my Golf, to replace the mat that destructive Daisy had devoured. There was no surprise to find, at the bottom of the box, a set of protective covers for Nick's new Mercedes, which had an even newer replacement engine, after it had become waterlogged in a deep flood in Ireland a month after delivery. We decided to take the new Golf to France, as William could alight with ease, mindful of last year when Nick took his Range Rover and we had to lift William in (I did my share after Nick cracked his ribs falling over his wallet), not just because the boot was so high, but because my perverse puppy flatly refused to jump.

This year was going to be different. William was now a strapping two-year-old, who could jump over the car if he so wished. He could hop in and out car as directed and would be much easier to handle. We were looking forward to our holiday with Wills.

This was my wish list for William's holiday behaviour this year:

He would walk well on the lead without pulling.
He would come immediately when called.
He would jump in and out of the car to order.
He would not hump other dogs.
He would not eat the leather sofa in the villa.
He would stay clean (a vain hope).

Last year, he was totally uncontrolled despite having been to puppy evening classes and a sophisticated Welsh boarding school:

He pulled the lead so strongly that our arms were wrenched out of their sockets.

He refused, just refused, to come back despite repeated calling and whistling.

He had to be airlifted into the boot (except on leaving the vet's, when he sprang in like Nureyev).

He did not go on humping sprees, because we kept him firmly on a lead in the presence of other dogs.

He was kept happily in a cage in the villa, which he identified as his home.

He loved getting muddy more than life itself; his worst mucky episode was when, on his birthday, he sat in a puddle of sump-oil and needed a professional French lavage (wash and fluff-up).

To get into training, I strapped William into his harness, donned my yellow rubber gloves and went on my monthly expedition clearing up the rubbish that had been abandoned in the lane, mostly in the lay-by, by courting couples who had nowhere else to go. I regularly saw two cars arrive, then a guy would emerge and look around surreptitiously before moving into the other car. I could understand why unhappily married folk had extra-marital affairs, but I had a problem with the picnic litter, soggy tissues and condoms that they left behind. Even worse, sometimes there were drug-users' needles left dangerously abandoned. Each time I saw some litter, I asked William to stop so that I could pick it up and place it into a plastic bag. He became so adept at this exercise that he halted abruptly when he saw any litter. It obviously offended him as much as it offended me!

My builders were very good at clearing up at the end of each day. In appreciation of their kindness, I gave them a large tin of chocolate fingers to enjoy with their many cups of coffee. I had already used two jars of decaffeinated coffee, one jar of normal-strength coffee, two pounds of sugar and a cow-full of milk. It made me smile when, later in the day, I spied that the master carpenter had commandeered the Cadbury's biscuit tin for his paintbrushes! The plumbers arrived and fitted a gleaming white bathroom and thankfully reconnected the hot water in the barn, as I had guests there for Christmas and the New Year.

I then turned my attention to packing for our holiday. I bought William a new metre-square piece of green bedding, a bag full of toys for Christmas costing only £9.99 and some food and liver bones to prevent him chewing any furniture. I found his passport and vaccination record. All he would need now was his bowls, some water for the journey, and some treats. Oh! - and his comb, harness, lead and a large William-coloured towel (new, with the label still attached). There would be little room in the VW for my suitcase, but as long as I took my passport, Barbour, boots, sheepskin hat and some Euros, I was happy, though at an exchange rate of one Euro to the pound, shopping may prove expensive.

Sue from Towsers kennels telephoned to invite me to present a book-reading (of *Barking Mad* not *Pump up!*) in the Roborough pub run by her son Alex and daughter-in-law Vicky. As public houses were suffering badly from the recession, Sue decided to put together a programme with an event each month to attract the regular and not-so-regular customers. I was the January girl, Johnny Kingdom was invited for February and the rest of the year was yet to be arranged. She promised a log fire, a pub-supper and an invitation for young William. How could I refuse! I was flattered and nervous in equal measure, as previously, I had only read out loud to my children and grandchildren. I started thinking of the passages that would amuse and, hopefully, entertain the group. There was the time when William nearly amputated my finger (though I chose not to relive this), the time when he pee-ed over Claire as she sunbathed in her bikini, which still makes me smile, the fateful day at Jeanine and Peter's house (where he caused chaos) had to be tops, but the incident from *William: Still Barking* where Wills joined forces with destructive Daisy to empty a feather cushion just had to be told.

CHAPTER 19

OFF TO FRANCE

NICK SAILED FROM Dublin to Fishguard then drove down to Devon arriving before dark. We were overjoyed to see him. Although Nick and I had been together many times during the year, Nick had not seen William since Christmas. They bonded like a father and son who had been apart far too long, although they had spoken regularly on the telephone! The next day, Nick cleaned the car and fitted my dog guard into his car together with the new black boot liners. We were ready to sail. Early that evening, Nick, Claire and I met Martin, Jo, Maggie and Charlie at The Chichester Arms for our Christmas celebrations and so that I could give the children their 'High School Musical' dolls (needless to say, their dizzy granny gave them the wrong dolls, so they had to swap them!), and their red velvet dresses with cream satin sashes to wear on Christmas Day. Apparently, they wore them for the whole day and refused to take them off!

We were sailing the next day from Portsmouth on the 11pm ferry, so took the drive from Barnstaple slowly with multiple breaks for William. We stopped for lunch in a non-descript pub for an even more non-descript bowl of soup, but in its favour, dogs were allowed. William immediately sprawled out and covered most of the pub floor and had to be restrained from removing the Christmas tree decorations before the big day. En route, most wooded places also had footpaths suitable for dog-walking; our favourite stopping-place was in Berwick St James, a delightful village just off the A303 with a perfect track across the fields where William could run free. Later, we opted for a pub supper in Portsmouth, where we sat in the window with a good view of William in the laden car.

Twenty years ago, on the way back from a lovely skiing holiday with Nick in Val d'Isère, we left his car outside our smart hotel under the care of the hotel doorman, taking in just our overnight bags. In the morning, to our horror we found the car completely stripped of everything except my anorak (what was wrong with my anorak?). The worst thing to be stolen was my address book; since then I have tried whenever possible to avoid leaving anything on view when leaving my car and I have always kept two address books. A year to the day, after a good deal of hassle, the insurance claim was eventually settled. I just hope that someone was able to enjoy using my beloved silk-lined shocking pink ski-suit!

We booked in an hour-and-a-half early at Portsmouth Docks. We showed our red passports and William's blue passport to the Brittany Ferries agent and gave her the car number. She did not scan the dog even though last year William was scanned at this point. She gave us tickets for our cabin and a yellow sticker for the car which stated 'PET ON BOARD' and displayed a picture of a dog kennel.

All was well until she asked: "Do you have a muzzle for your dog?"

"No, I did not think it necessary," I replied. She then handed me a black muzzle to be used when we took William up to the top deck for his overnight stay. He was given a 'Museliere Nylon' size 3. The snout sizes varied according to the breed of dog:

Chien miniature - Pinsher – Yorkshire
Caniche nain – Teckel – Westies – Cairn – Whippet
Cocker – Caniche – Fox Terrier
Doberman – Berger allemande
Dogue - St Bernard – Terre-Neuve
4XL Montagne des Pyrénées – Saint-Hubert
Rottweiller – Dogue Anglais
5XL Dogue de Bordeaux
Boxers (Spécial museaux courts)

We left William in the car until we were called; meanwhile we found our cabin and settled in. Almost immediately, there was an announcement: "Please could all dog owners who wish to leave their dogs in kennels assemble by the lift where they will be accompanied up to the top deck". After a considerable struggle (rounds one, two, three and four to William; round five to us!), the muzzle was fitted properly and we entered the lift to join eight embarrassed black-nosed dogs, all much daintier than Wills. There was no fighting, no barking, just soulful, pleading eyes peering over all the muzzles. On the top floor William was put in a large clean kennel with a fitted food and water bowl, given his new rug and settled down for the night. There was rather a commotion from one lady who had clearly underestimated her dog's girth and booked a small kennel. "I will never get my dog in there," she exclaimed, and pleaded to be given a large one. We left abruptly, hoping that her dog would be allocated more comfortable quarters.

Fortunately, it was a calm crossing to St Malo and we slept well. In the morning there was an announcement, just a tad early at 5.30am: "Please can all those people with dogs in kennels kindly collect them". We went up to the top deck, where all the dog owners were allowing their dogs to pee on the deck. It was a great bonus for William to be able to relieve himself prior to our long journey to Morlaix.

CHAPTER 20

A NOT-SO-PERFECT CHRISTMAS

WE ARRIVED AT Le Manoir de Coat Amour converted stables to find that the villa had been artistically decorated by Stafford and Jenny with a Christmas tree packed full of lights and trinkets and the table laid for a romantic dinner for two with a bottle of Champagne in the refrigerator. We set out for Leclerc supermarket to purchase some initial provisions (Nick even had his Leclerc trolley token, which he had squirreled away since last year!). After lunch, Nick crashed out totally exhausted from the arduous journey, so I took William down the lane which had formerly been the track of the Roscoff-Concarneau railway. I walked 1.9 kilometres of the Morlaix-Carhaix section with Wills on the lead, then turned and headed for home. What a difference from last year! There was no pulling, no leaping up when anyone passed; instead he stood still expectantly waiting for a stroke from each person who came towards us. I was so proud of him; what a difference a year had made. At last I had a dog, who not only looked good, but was obedient. I was proud of him.

Unfortunately, William was unable to rekindle his friendship with Stafford and Jenny's dog, Phoebe, as she was 'on heat' and kept firmly indoors. When Nick was bringing wood into the villa, William escaped; it did not need a degree in canine behavior to discover where he would be. We found him staring at Phoebe through the glass in the front door of the Manoir, salivating like a dog possessed, before he rushed round the back of the house to try and gain a rear entry. Sadly there was not going to be an Anglo-French alliance as Phoebe was going back to Le Chien et l'Enfant organisation for another possible mating. William was not pleased; he was hoping to have all his Christmases at once deep inside the delectable Phoebe. We spent a delightful evening dining with Stafford and Jenny at the Manoir before they left Morlaix to spend time with family and friends, leaving William bereft with only the tantalizing aroma of unrequited love.

The next day we decided to take William to our favourite beach west of the Horn river close to Sibiril. The beach was cold and deserted; we were muffled up in hats and gloves but pleased to enjoy one of the most beautiful beaches in Brittany. Wills leapt out of the car, down the bank to the beach to become a puppy again. He dug holes, performed headstands and a variety of well-choreographed forward, sideways and backward flips, always under our feet to make sure he had a captive audience, until he was covered in a wet layer of sand and seaweed. Then he noticed some geese floating happily in the bay, and with a series of streamlined bounds resembling a winning racehorse smoothly pacing the final furlong, he was in the water just in time to see the flock become airborne and drift gracefully and effortlessly away. He then felt silly and looked around for something else, anything else, to chase. We walked around the corner to another stunning bay with William leading the way, always in front but always keeping close to us. It was a joy to be a family again; William had his proud mother and father with him and like all doting parents, we were there for him. The icy wind bit, my chest started to tighten, so we walked back to the car, lifted the hatch-back up for a happy, sandy dog to jump in. Last year, we had to capture the beast, put his front paws on the boot, then lift him in – life was so much easier this time.

After William's feverish dancing on the beach, we noticed that part of his identity disc was missing; the Perspex cover and telephone number had become detached and was lost on the sands. We popped into a pet shop and purchased a metal cylinder tag, wrote his details on the slither of paper and screwed it firmly home.

The following day we decided to try to find the beach to the east of the Horn river close to Brenesquen. We twisted our way around a number of winding lanes until we found a lane with grass growing down the centre, which came to a dead end. We parked and let William out to explore for us. There was a white sandy route alongside the river as it meandered in exaggerated loops towards the sea; it was a perfectly safe place for dogs to roam free. William was in seventh heaven. His erect furry tail fanned out in the sea breeze, so that it was two feet in height and a foot in width; from the back he looked every inch a proud peacock performing a look-at-me courting display. Nick and I were his only fan club; there was no Phoebe, no female retriever, not even a cross-bred, willing bitch. The wind blew icier, so we walked back to the car by a sheltered forest path (deserted, apart from one spaniel and a jogger, who unfortunately found me squatting!), happy to have discovered another favourite walk.

I had to admit to Nick that I had a chest infection. I had been bravely walking in below-freezing weather, muffled up in my cozy sheepskin hat and gloves and my Barbour jacket but I found it impossible to get warm. The villa was as cold as the weather outside; the log fire did nothing to penetrate such low temperatures. I started coughing and sneezing until I was exhausted. I moved out of the double-bed to give Nick some peace, but he only worried about me and was unable to sleep. The rest of the holiday, I stayed in another bedroom in order to give myself the freedom to cough and spit into tissues or sit up and read. It was not a happy holiday.

I diagnosed my chest infection as pneumonia as I was expectorating green sputum, plus a severe sinus infection with similarly-coloured gunge, which made lying flat at night well-nigh impossible. Nick announced that if I went to a French docteur, I would be given antibiotic suppositories. I decided to fight the infection and cure myself! I later found out from my friend Ann, who lives in France, that French medicine is now similar to British medicine in every way. I could have had oral antibiotics.

This wretched illness reminded me of the time when I was working in hospital as a young physiotherapist, forty-odd years ago, and our job was to encourage the chest patients to cough up their sputum. This was done by tipping our patients so that their head was lower than their feet into the correct position for postural drainage. We helped to loosen their secretions in readiness for expectorating by clapping and vibrating their chests; an offering of phlegm in the sputum pot gave us immediate job satisfaction! For years, we carried a bleep and were on an 'On Call Rota' for chest patients with the possibility of being called in the evenings, nights or at weekends. Eventually the large sterilized silver sputum pots with lift-up-lids were replaced by smaller disposable plastic pots. The worst mistake I ever made as a young physiotherapist was when I dropped a full sputum pot onto the floor of the ward! An accident I will never forget, and one that was impossible to clear up. Nowadays it is much more acceptable to spit into tissues, unless a sample is needed for pathology.

Nick was wonderful; he willingly undertook shopping, cooking, fire-lighting and dog-walking duties. He should have won the highest award for his consummate nursing, care and concern. He was amazingly helpful; he felt under the weather too, but dosed himself with the best quality wine as a prophylactic!

One day, Nick drove me to Binic to a favourite shop of ours which sold warm jumpers. Before we entered the shop, we decided to explore a beach that we had only seen previously through a passage-way close to the quay. We muffled up and let William foot-loose and fancy-free to perfect his cartwheel routine, undaunted by the icy sea-breeze. We were the only people on the beach. Suddenly my bravery deserted me, so I whispered to Nick that I was freezing and would return to the car, leaving Nick to watch my mad dog's display all the way to the rocks on the other side of the beach. Suddenly Wills turned and saw that I was not there; he dashed at break-neck speed, like a puppy possessed, for the passage-way despite Nick calling and whistling for the 'bastard' (Nick's word!) to come back. By this time, I was warm in the car reading the Brittany guide book, when I became aware of a very furry, fawn tail circling the car. I leapt out. William was in danger in the road, completely fazed by not having found me. After this incident, we decided that either we would walk together, or if I felt too unwell, Nick would take William out on his own.

Nick kindly took on duties for William's first and last daily trips outside, when he was taken out on a lead in the dark to fulfill his call to nature. Nick was so tuned in to hearing the first 'woof', and leaping out of bed so as not to wake me in my sickroom, that one morning he undertook his duty only to find William hell-bent on chasing a marmalade cat. It was

2.55am! The next morning Nick gave me a full and frank report of the 'bastard's' nocturnal activities.

My chest and sinus infection worsened and with it my appetite for life's pleasures; I went off chocolate, fruit, vegetables, alcohol and, for the first time ever, any fulfillment of our love (I was too ill to tango!). All I wanted was clear, consommé broth, which, surprisingly, considering it was a French recipe, was unavailable at Leclerc supermarket. We bought a selection of soups together with soft and hard cough pastilles, guaranteed to soothe the sorest throat and more importantly, prevent the dreaded paroxysms of nocturnal coughing.

While we were at the supermarket, despite being left with a liver-filled bone, William investigated the Christmas tree. We had previously removed the chocolate figures, knowing that it was dangerous for dogs to eat chocolate, but William completely decimated one dangling dolly, which could have been anything from a fairy to a gremlin, and chewed up one of the glass lights. Fortunately, we had unplugged the lights early on, so there was no danger of electrocution, but we were unsure about how much glass he had eaten; we hoped that he had spat it out with the same disdain that he had shown for his distasteful worming pill. We went to a selection of supermarkets and electrical shops to find a spare bulb without success; eventually, when we had almost given up the search, we were relieved to find some in a large garden centre.

On Christmas Eve, I felt well enough to visit Ploumanac'h, where William walked among the boulders but kept to the path. Last year, he was on the lead, but tugged and pulled in an attempt to get free. He was so strong and wilful that we curtailed our walk before our shoulders were ripped out of their sockets. This year, he was a dream; he met other walkers who stroked him and other dogs who played with him, but always came back when he was called. What a difference a year made! I was so proud of him.

We visited the beautiful kitchen shop in Peros Guirec, where I was able to buy Nick a unique kitchen clock that he had been admiring; they even gift-wrapped it for me. Then we popped into the antique shop on the hill to find that the beautiful bronze sculpture of a John Dory fish which we had seen last year, was still there. "Would you like it for Christmas?" Nick asked me. "I should love it," I replied. "But where would it look best?" Nick generously bought me my namesake, saying that we could decide where to put it when we arrived home. That evening, Nick cooked a freshly-caught John Dory, which despite its ugliness was an exceptionally tasty fish. Nick is a much better cook than I am; he is adventurous and enjoys the whole experience from creating the recipe to producing a delicious dish, usually with a glass of wine in one hand! Later, he gave me an apron printed with the immortal words: 'I kiss better than I cook"!

We drove to many of the haunts that we had enjoyed so much last year; we lunched at Paimpol, where my appetite deserted me, and visited the kitchen shops at Landivisiau and Landerneau. At the last town, we walked William to heel along the Elorn river and compared him favourably with the inquisitive, tugging, disobedient puppy that we tried so hard to control the previous year. At Huelgoat, the weather was too cold and inhospitable to reach the glorious boulders, so we spent the minimum amount of time outside, just enough time for William to have a walk (and lose the barrel of his screw-on identity tag!), before rushing back to the warmth of the car. Bravely, we tried to enjoy ourselves, but everything was a struggle as we felt so tired and ill. It was a disappointing holiday. I thanked Nick for being, as always, so devoted, caring and loving; he had done everything he could possibly have done to ease my discomfort. I adored him.

CHAPTER 21

HOMEWARD BOUND

AFTER SUCH A disastrous holiday, we could not wait to get home. This year, we made sure to remember the French vet's appointment (it had to be made 24 to 48 hours prior to sailing), by writing a large notice "VET 4.30pm WEDNESDAY". This became the most important date on our calendar! We kept checking to see if we knew which day of the week it was that day! When the time eventually arrived, William bounded in, leapt onto the couch (at the third attempt), had his microchip scanned and received a sachet of anti-tick lotion on the back of his neck close to his skin. Then, I was amazed as the vet prized his mouth open and pushed an anti-worm tablet down his throat. William was too shocked to fight, it all happened so quickly. This brave man then stamped and signed William's blue passport, which certified him fit to travel. The appointment cost €46.50 or £46.50 at today's exchange rate. We now hoped that our sailing would not be cancelled, otherwise we would have to repeat this appointment (and pay again). This would have been tricky, if not impossible, as the next day was New Year's Day, when the vet would be closed for the holiday.

The departure day eventually arrived and, despite both feeling unwell, we managed to leave the villa clean and tidy and, importantly, the well-watered Christmas tree alive and flourishing. It was the only thing that thrived in the intense cold! Nick packed the car while William became increasingly disturbed. We took him, en route to Roscoff, to his favourite beach near Sibil to let off some energy. He went wild, leaving none of the virgin sand without a print of some part of his anatomy. He had rehearsed in France for this occasion for two weeks and gave the performance of his life; his 'break dancing' would have won an award purely for its originality. He gyrated his body so that every bit in turn, from his nose to his tail, carved out swathes of sand leaving a uniquely sculptured canvas. In this intensive process, the artist was so wedded to his art that he neglected his own beauty; he became smeared with wet sand, his deep brown eyes happily peering out from a soggy, sand-drenched form that we knew to be called 'William'.

Nick took him for a walk across the fields in an attempt to shake off some of the sand, then toweled him down, as best he could, before letting him leap into the car. Then William amazed us. Knowing that his holiday had ended, he refused to jump into the vehicle; he put his front paws onto the boot and defiantly refused to move. He looked at both of us to register a 'one dog protest' in the only way he knew how; he did not wish his holiday to end. Nick folded him up and gently lifted him into the boot. He was coming home.

We drove to the Terminal Building of Brittany Ferries at Roscoff and presented one sandy dog, one pet passport, and our tickets to the male Receptionist. He gave me a hand-held ultra-sound to scan William's chip and checked the vet's entry in his passport; all was in order so we were given a round pink sticker for the car windscreen which stated clearly in capital letters 'PET ON BOARD' with a large black paw imprint. We let William have a last pee before joining the lane of esteemed dog-owners all preparing to board. We waited and waited; our 3.30pm deadline came and went, while we were still waiting on the windy quayside. Nick went into the terminal to find out the reason for the delay; he was told that the incoming ferry was delayed due to bad weather. Fortunately, knowing that I was a bad sailor, he did not relate this to me.

Eventually, about an-hour-and-a-half after our sailing time, we boarded and made our way to our cabin. Wills stayed in the boot with the car windows open and the car alarm de-activated. Unfortunately, there were no kennels on this crossing. I tucked into bed, after apologising to Nick for being such poor company, and slept most of the trip. We arrived in Plymouth at midnight in need of diesel and some immediate sustenance, so we were fortunate to find a late-night Tesco's, which provided fuel for the car and chicken sandwiches for the three of us. They were William's favourite; he was happy again! We arrived home at 1.30am absolutely shattered from the journey, which could have been fun if we had only felt better.

The house was cold; I had left the heating on continuously but only on a low heat. When I turned the boiler up to maximum, the heat took ages to penetrate, as it was so bitter outside. The next morning, I telephoned my Aga service engineer and begged him to come over and kindly light the stove for me, but this became a mammoth task as the oil pump had seized and needed a night of lubrication. How I identified with the oil pump! Nick kindly filled my refrigerator with food, bought more cough syrup, walked William, cooked dinner, and insisted that I telephone the GP. The next day he left for another ferry trip to Ireland, where the house he was having converted into a 'Grand Design' was almost ready for occupation. He apologised that he could not take William with him, as it was not yet dog-friendly; the essential (heated) outdoor shower had been fitted but the kennel was, as yet, unfinished.

The guests who were staying in my Barn over New Year complained that they had been cold; I was not surprised as the weather was below freezing. "We had to spend £40 on logs to keep warm," they commented sadly. I commiserated with them and reimbursed their fuel bill, as I knew how awful it was to feel cold on holiday.

The next day, I had a telephone appointment with my GP and was prescribed amoxicillin for 5 days; he kindly said that I could have the prescription sent to my address by the Home Delivery Service. Nothing happened! The next day, Lloyds Pharmacy apologised for the error and kindly made sure that I was their first delivery that day. Gradually, over the next week, I started feeling less ill. William suffered by not having his daily walks, but he was allowed to romp in the garden four times a day and seemed to enjoy playing with Oakley, the Jack Russell who came to work with Dave, the Master Carpenter. Oakley was always kept on a lead; William would tease him by springing towards him and then leaping away out of reach. It was a typically cat and mouse game but it certainly kept the feline side of William amused.

While I was languishing in bed, I was telephoned by the receptionist from the Nuffield Hospital in Taunton to see why I had not appeared for my clinic. I was distraught to think that I had let my patients down, but, in my ill state, I had not even opened my 2009 diary. "Please could you apologise to my patients, let them know that I am unwell with pneumonia and kindly rebook them for me," I uttered, full of remorse. Things had to improve.

When, Barry, my gardener, came to a frost-hardened garden, I asked him if he would kindly help Dave to move my book-shelves and files into the new office in the Barn. Dave fitted the office out while Barry carried the many books and files. I felt too ill to comment when my gardener brought across a pile of text-books with the book titled *Vibrators* enticingly laid on the top. I also refused to rise to the challenge when he carried over a drawer containing a small dumbbell suitable for exercising the penis, which Nick and I had found in a Norwegian sex-shop. At least my sense of humour had not deserted me, even though I was too off-colour to share it!

Nick telephoned daily from Ireland to see if I was improving; it took another week before I started feeling more like myself. My daughter, Claire, wanted to come down from London to look after me, but I did not want her to catch this bug; my friend, Judy, offered to look after me, but I refused to let her come in case I infected her.

I did attend Jenny Metcalfe's funeral at Pilton Parish Church. Dick, from the tennis club, collected me, otherwise I would not have been able to go. Despite having menthol throat sweets, I had a coughing fit during the Eulogy, which was made worse by my acute embarrassment. A kind soul brought me a glass of water, which instantly cured this uncalled-for attack. Jenny's service was a celebration of a special and unique life, which blended her spiritual healing skills with her intriguing wander-lust. The beautiful church was stone cold, but warmed by family, friends and colleagues all queuing to sign the book of condo-lences, and donate money in her name to Fremington Children's Hospice. I was pleased that I had shared the day with Jenny's friends, but even more pleased to jump back into bed!

On Saturday, my son Martin kindly telephoned for a shop-ping list. I gave him a list of provisions to last a week, carefully listed in order for ease of shopping at Tesco's. However, Martin shops at Sainsbury's because he considers them to have more ethical trading standards. I was most grateful for this help and thanked Martin for kindly bringing in my shopping for me. My choice of food and lack of anything green obviously left much to be desired, as he quipped: "As your dietician, I do not think you are having enough fruit and vegetables!". He then introduced me to grey, not-so-soft, recycled lavatory paper (I like any paper that touches my intimate zone to be as pure as my soap!).

This scratchy paper took me back more than fifty years, when my grandfather Blundell, who lived in Halstead, Kent, tore up newspaper and threaded string through the corner to make toilet paper for use in the cold (and spidery) outside lavatory. It was useless! After putting up with newspaper, and then many years of scratchy paper that was 'Medicated with Izal Germicide' - and totally non-absorbent – my guests and I deserve the best and softest paper on the market, not stuff recycled from yesterday's newspapers. Then this re-constituted paper acted like a scorpion with a sting in its tail; it refused to dissolve and blocked up my loo. So now I had a plethora of previously published papier mâché in my pan!

Martin brought Bob round for William to play with and enjoy some much needed exercise. It looked more like war than a playful game, but both survived the wrestling holds, the kickboxing and the multiple tumbling, though it seemed as if Bob had unlimited puppy energy and could go on for at least another ten rounds! William slunk into the kitchen, exhausted!

Jo and the girls had thoughtfully made some delicious broccoli and stilton soup, and Maggie and Charlie had made me a beautifully-coloured card, designed to speed my recovery. It seemed as if my friends were also very concerned about my failing health; I received telephone calls from my daughter Claire, my brother Alan, my sister Joyce, and friends Judy, Kay, and Ann (from France). I also had a Skype call from Dorothy, and emails from cousin Claire and my friends, Liz and Ann.

Three weeks to the day, I started to feel better; my head cleared sufficiently for me to want to attack *The Daily Telegraph* crossword (even though I found it more difficult than normal!). I started to get bored, so I wrote about William's trip to France. It now seemed possible that I would be well enough to run my clinic in two days time. Life was looking up.

CHAPTER 22

FUNNY VALENTINE

AFTER I HAD BEEN back from France for 10 days, I felt well enough to walk William down the lane. He looked at me incredulously, when I showed him his harness; he could not believe his luck. The weather had turned much milder and the winter sun had made a welcome and timely appearance; it was lovely, just lovely to see a clear blue sky. William stuck to me like glue; he kept looking up at me to make sure that I was still there. Fortunately he spent so much time sniffing that the walk was not arduous, and I was able to breathe without puffing on the return journey back up the hill to my cottage. This seemed a milestone for me and certainly heralded my recovery.

I was sent a warning email from Sue Blackmore, the owner of Towsers kennels. It read: "There is a danger with a pink dimpled ball containing a bell, with only one hole. Your dog could get his tongue stuck inside due to suction.". Apparently, a Labrador/cross in America had been unable to withdraw his tongue, which had swollen, become gangrenous and needed amputation. I looked at William's green dimpled ball and found it had a hole each end; I took no chances, though I knew I was over-reacting as I threw it in the bin.

My next job was to select the chapters of *Barking Mad in Barnstaple* that would entertain the customers attending my book-reading at The New Inn at Roborough. Various incidents in William's eventful life had to be told, so I selected extracts from Chapters 1, 4, 5 and 12 from *Barking Mad* followed by Chapter 1 of my new book *William: Still Barking*, as a taster. I emailed Steve Pugsley, Chairman of Halsgrove Publishers to ask for 30 copies of *Barking Mad* for the Book-reading. He was pleased to inform me that William's book had sold 400 copies to date (550 including the books that I had sold); Steve reckoned this was an extremely encouraging start, against a generally troubled market. I was delighted, particularly as the title of the book seemed to attract interest mostly among the local book-shops in Barnstaple (and from neighbouring Bideford, where the locals like to think that we in Barnstaple are indeed barking mad!).

I drove to Roborough with Glennis and a very excitable William, by a tortuous route encompassing all the winding lanes in Devon, which were covered in mud with dangerous ditches on both sides. It seemed as if we were driving over recently ploughed fields. I parked outside the New Inn and opened the boot ready to attach William's lead. He had other ideas; he leapt out of the car before I could catch him and ran into the road. Mercifully a car stopped abruptly, and I was able to drag him kicking and screaming into the pub. "William has arrived!" some wag announced. I bought some raffle tickets and overheard someone quipping: "I'm not buying any raffle tickets if the prize is William!"

I was led over to a winged chair by the fire, reminiscent of the one that Ronnie Corbett used for his fireside chats though, thankfully, my feet were able to reach the floor. I was faced by a circle of about twenty experienced dog-lovers. I was introduced by Sue's beautiful daughter-in-law, Vicky, and started to read from Chapter 1 to set the scene. The audience loved it and tittered in all the right places; I enjoyed reading my work out loud much more than I had expected, and hoped that I had conveyed the sentiments appropriately with the required amount of drama, but without going over the top. We then had a break for a delicious supper while the raffle was drawn. It was my lucky day; I won 15Kg of dog-food, a bag that I was unable to pick up, but which Shaun kindly lifted into my car.

After supper, I read the 'feather incident' from *William: Still Barking* while some of the audience giggled as they obviously identified with this visual scenario. Glennis asked me to read 'Afterthoughts' from *Barking Mad*, I think, just to hear me say: "Glennis was right"! At the end of the evening, two ladies asked if I would come to Braunton for another book-reading, as their husbands had been unable to attend. As I had enjoyed the evening so much, I readily agreed and handed over my business card for them to make arrangements. After the reading, some of the group brought in their own copies of William's book for me to sign, whilst others bought a signed copy. We asked the best way home and were directed to a wide, mud-free, ditch-free road which climbed up close to the radio mast above Torrington. On this high ground it began to snow with white fluffy flakes reminiscent of William and Daisy's feather fight; the snow settled and the drive home became increasingly tricky, but I was consoled to think that everyone had enjoyed the evening. The pub was filled with laughter and the hero, Wills, had won a gigantic bag of his favourite chicken nuts.

On Valentine's Day 2009, I had owned William for two years. He had arrived as an adventurous ten-week-old puppy, who very definitely had a mind of his own. This strong will, together with the strength of a bull-elephant and the speed of a frightened gazelle, had enabled him to play havoc in a number of unforeseen ways and with increasing and exasperating regularity. He had grown at an alarming rate, having secretly enlisted for the Charles Atlas muscle training course. He was sent to puppy-training classes and then away to boarding school in an effort to make him behave like an angel. Over the past two years, he had gradually became more obedient, but throughout this intensive training, he never lost the huge capacity he had for wanting to be close to me and enjoying all the stroking, fondling and tummy-tickles on offer.

I was so grateful to Nick for generously giving me William for Christmas in 2006, and even though everyone knows that 'a dog is not just for Christmas', there were times when I (and my family) thought that I would not be able to cope with such a gigantic, headstrong hound and that we would have to re-home him. Fortunately, with regular training and a firm body-harness, we have weathered the storm and now I have the most affectionate, loveable dog, whom I adore. He has a unique, and at times, over-excitable temperament, which scares the heck out of my visitors, but he has a character all his own, which vacillates from maddening monster, right through to the cuddly cutie that we know as 'William'. To Nick and me, he is truly the best.

He is our funny Valentine.

AFTERTHOUGHTS

My wish list for William's holiday behaviour this year:

He would walk well on the lead without pulling.
He scored 10/10 this year. How amazingly different from last year!

He would come immediately when called.
He scored 9/10 this year, which was a fine achievement. He lost one point at Binic Beach, when he left Nick to search for me.

He would jump in and out of the car to order.
He scored 9/10 for jumping in to order. One point was lost on the last day when, understandably, he did not want to leave France. He scored an impressive 10/10 for jumping out of the car.

He would not hump other dogs.
He would have dearly liked to father some little Phoebes, but he was not given the opportunity. Sadly for William, he scored 10/10 - though I have the feeling that he would rather have scored ten times!

He would not eat the leather sofa in the villa.
He scored 10/10 for not eating the leather sofa, but marred his record by munching a Christmas tree decoration and a Christmas tree light.

He would stay clean (a vain hope).
He scored 0/10 for keeping his fur clean. He caked it with sand at every opportunity and brought most of the beach into the boot of the car! We knew this would happen, as this was

one of his less endearing traits, but all part of that loveable chap we call 'William'.

Is William still barking?

When we were in France, William suddenly spotted a stone elephant, one of an exquisite pair that graced the steps to the impressive Manoir de Coat Amour; he suddenly barked loudly and leapt upwards and backwards in one startled movement. My mammoth dog was scared of an elephant half his size!

At home, William still has his moments; he will bark excitedly if someone comes to the door. He will also bark if a horse trots by or if a cat decides to walk past. He barks to go out first thing in the morning and barks to come back inside. I am still fazed when he barks at night – like the night when he barked at 2am because he heard gunshots.

Would I have another puppy?

No way! I could not go through the puppy stage again. NEVER. However, I firmly believe that our bond is stronger because we have been together for the whole of William's life.

Would I have been better to take in a rescue dog?

Maybe, but this was a steep learning curve. I had always wanted a puppy, so I have achieved my dream. I had no idea that dog training would be such hard work and so frustrating. Two years later, I have the dog that I would have loved initially. If I had given a home to a trained dog, would we have been as close?

Does William enhance my life?

William is my soul-mate, my companion and my friend, who has enhanced my life and given me unequivocal loyalty, love and devotion. It is a privilege to own such a handsome dog with such a unique, impish character. He is a giant among dogs; gentle and sensitive. Unashamedly, I love him.

WILLIAM'S PEDIGREE

WILLIAM	PARENTS	GRANDPARENTS
Seruilia Snowball	SIRE Gatchells Lone Ranger	SIRE **Show Champion** Marjamez Midnight Cowboy At Westervane
		DAM **SW Show Champion** Dewmist Serenella (Imp Swe)
	DAM Bedeslea Blushing Bride Via Seruilia	SIRE Seruilia Steamroller Stan
		DAM Bedeslea Black Eyed Susan

BY THE SAME AUTHOR

Barking Mad in Barnstaple The diary of a Professor of Physiotherapy who was given a fluffy Golden Retriever puppy by her nearest and dearest for Christmas and who adamantly believed that puppy training was easy and would produce the perfect dog. William remained uncontrolled despite diligently attending all the dog training classes available in Devon and the surrounding Counties.

Clench it or Drench it! Self-help book for women with urinary leakage

Love Your Gusset: Making friends with your pelvic floor Cartoon book for women with incontinence, sexual dysfunction and an outrageous sense of humour

Make it or Fake it! Self-help book for women with sexual dysfunction

Prevent it! Guide for men and women with leakage from the back passage

Use it or Lose it! Self-help book for men with urinary leakage and erectile dysfunction

Living and Loving After Prostate Surgery Self-help book for men with incontinence and erectile dysfunction after prostate surgery

Stronger and Longer! Guide on improving erections with pelvic floor exercises

Pump Up Your Penis: Easy exercises to strengthen your erection Cartoon book for men with erectile dysfunction and a wild sense of humour.

Pelvic Dysfunction in Men: Diagnosis and Treatment of Male Incontinence and Erectile Dysfunction Textbook

Pelvic floor exercises for erectile dysfunction Textbook

All books are available from
www.yourpelvic floor.co.uk

AUTHOR

Grace Dorey is a Consultant Physiotherapist at Nuffield Hospital, Taunton and The Queen Street Medical Centre, Barnstaple. She also works at North Devon District NHS Hospital, Barnstaple. She is Emeritus Professor of Physiotherapy (Urology) at the University of the West of England, Bristol, UK.